JOURNEY FROM MIDNIGHT

A true story of tragedy and Trauma, overcome by resilience and determination after falling through the cracks of the system.

By

Selira V. Samanne

VOLUME ONE

First Edition
Printed in the United States of America

ISBN: 978-1-7368763-1-2

AUTHOR'S MESSAGE

This is a work of creative nonfiction. All of the events in this book are true to the author's memory. Some names and identifying features may have been changed to protect the identity of certain parties. The author in no way represents any company, corporation, or brand, mentioned herein. The views expressed in this book are solely those of the author.

DISCLAIMER

Any information contained in the following pages is considered accurate and truthful. The following information is presented purely for informative purposes. This book is designed to provide information, education and motivation to readers. It is sold with the understanding that the publisher and author are not engaged to render any type of psychological, legal, or any other professional advice. The content within is the sole expression and opinion of its author. No guarantees are expressed or implied. You are responsible for your own choices, actions and results.

TABLE OF CONTENTS

EPITAPH

After A While
After a while you learn
The subtle difference between
Holding a hand and chaining a soul
And you learn that love doesn't mean leaning
And company doesn't always mean
Security
And you begin to learn
That kisses aren't contracts
And presents aren't promises
And you begin to accept your defeats
With your head up and your eyes ahead
With the grace of a woman
Not the grief of a child
And you learn
To build all your roads on today
Because tomorrow's ground
Is too uncertain for plans
And futures have a way of falling down
in mid-flight
After a while you learn
That even sunshine burns
if you get too much
So you plant your own garden
And decorate your own soul
Instead of waiting for someone
To bring you flowers
And you learn
That you really can endure
And you realize
That you really do have worth
And you learn and you learn
With every goodbye you learn
Veronica Shoffstalll

VIII

RUNAWAY TRAIN

The time is now for those who have been abused, abandoned and forgotten from very young, to be seen and given a genuine helping hand up. We have to hear, acknowledge and support the children, teens and young adults who are suffering worse on the streets than the environments they ran away from.

Sometimes going back to what was once called home, may not even feel like a viable option. It makes you want to believe you could have a better life, in some better place.

In this book, drawing from my story, I would like the primary focus to spotlight first and foremost: the runaways and abused children who have to choose the unknown, and at times, treacherous streets to survive. My story defines situations that so many runaways and homeless youth may still find themselves in, while having to cope with the problems, people and environments that go along with them. This book can give them the chance to identify with someone who can relate with first hand experience and learn there is hope for a decent life after surviving on the streets.

I would like to give the world a glimpse into the life of a former runaway. I was a child lost on a lonesome path, trying to reach a better place. I was led to make many adult decisions that would most likely have been made differently had I been armed with knowledge and a stable home environment. I would also like to help readers find options to turn the bad into something good from within one's self.

This book is for those looking for happiness along the way, which can sometimes guide us through our darkest hours. It is my greatest wish to be a shining beacon to re-inform and re-educate the world of the long term, devastating effects of child abuse: sexual, physical, emotional and neglect.

More often than not, this abuse can lead to many adulthood dysfunctional patterns, such as run-ins with the police, criminal activity and chronic homelessness. This behavior could continue on throughout their entire adult lives. Many victims of abuse are incarcerated women and men who have carried on the legacy of abuse; unable to process through the darkness.

It is my hope to shed light on those children, teens and adults who find themselves still lost in the dark. Many lose themselves and never find their way back after they resort to crimes and other forms of self sabotage. Unhealthy addictions can lead them to feel like they want to give up completely and feel there is no way back.

Native American children and teens who are subjected to living out in the middle of nowhere and have nowhere to go, must cope with extreme drug and alcohol abuse. Poverty, generational oppression, and constant gang-related drug devastation on designated Reservations take more drastic measures to cope with the severe abuse. They commit suicide.

Each year, an estimated 4.2 million youth and young adults experience homelessness. 700,000 of which are unaccompanied minors. Kids become lost with no one to help them. In America alone, the rate of missing, exploited and trafficked children grows each and every day. At least five children die each day from abuse. In 2021, 1,820 children died from abuse and neglect in America. 80% of child fatalities involve at least one parent.

Runaways are in search of a better way of life. What could be encountered is the complete opposite: homelessness, starvation, gangs, slavery, along with the worst possible extreme of death. The statistics of favorable outcomes are few: 70% of homeless youth leave home to escape pain and suffering. In the last year, three out of four homeless youth were victims of a crime. Almost 48% of female homeless youth have been the victim of a sexual assault. 70% of youth on the streets eventually become victims of some form of commercial sexual exploitation.

LGBTQ youth are overrepresented in the homeless youth population with as many as 40% of the nation's homeless youth being LGBTQ. Nearly 7 in 10 LGBTQ homeless youth find themselves without a home because of a lack of acceptance of their sexual orientation or gender identity.

An overwhelming amount of male and female runaways are susceptible to sex trafficking along with the worst possible horror of sex slavery. They could also be forced into prostitution on any scale. Sometimes, they make the choice to turn to that age-old profession in order to survive and maybe even thrive with whatever they think is safe and comfortable. The apparent risks of a pimp may seem transparent.

With readily available clientele in the masses and even more so now with the Dark Web, child sex slaves really do exist and are easily accessible for disturbed people of all ages. They exploit children with all the dazzling allures of security that easily dismiss the dangers for those kids merely wanting to survive.
60% of youth that are homeless are products of the foster care system. Statistics show 1 in 3 young people in foster care become homeless the day they reach 18 and age out.

Consuming hard drugs and alcohol in order to cope can lead to falling prey to all kinds of bad decisions and addictions. There are people who have no interest other than to use whatever you have left to give. It can leave you less of a person than you started out to be. In the end, they give up hope of ever getting back to good. The good they always dreamed of right from the beginning.

This is the story of my life and how I overcame the obstacles that were placed before me. From the life lessons I have acquired until now, I have reached my destination before I continue on. With the knowledge gained of what the journey has created within me, I now know where the road will lead next.

I would like to donate a portion of the proceeds from this book to fund:

THE JFM H.A.V.E.N. FOUNDATION

Helping
Adolescents and Adults
Validate
Every
Need

Thank you in advance for helping to share these words with those you feel could gain a bright light of insight and understanding. By sending this message out to those you know who are genuinely concerned, just like you. This unacceptable and atrocious oversight in America and around the world cannot go on.

With your support and genuine caring, we can rally this cause by making sure new Laws and Bills are created to protect some of the most vulnerable members of our society.

They can not stand alone anymore. We have to do our part as human beings to work together and truly come up with adequate solutions. I already have a good amount of good ideas to suggest but I cannot do it alone. I am ready to take my stand and insist on change.

Will you join me?

DEDICATION

This book is dedicated to my children. May I give them the gift of understanding.

SPECIAL NOTE

Music has always been an integral and meaningful part of my life. I decided to name each chapter with a meaningful hard rock song title. As you join me on this journey, I hope you enjoy the added rock music playlist that made up the soundtrack of my life, as the songs carried me a little further down the road. Each carefully curated and selected song reflects not only the years but also expresses the music that at times, kept my soul alive.

HELL IS FOR CHILDREN

I wrote this book with the ultimate quest for healing in mind. I knew by putting my story down on these pages, I could make most of the mysteries in my life make sense. In order for me to convey one of my biggest mysteries I must give a brief summary of how my story began. I was born in 1969 and despite all the hippies and flower children that made Make-Love-Not-War their mantra, the world was filled with sights of war and violence everywhere it seemed. The Vietnam War permeated the news, along with ignorance and prejudice because of skin color.

Though it was in upstate New York, I like to believe I was in my mother's womb at Woodstock, that summer in August. The massive event always fascinated me, which then made me more curious to learn any information I could find out about myself. For the entirety of my life up until that moment, the only thing I knew was the place of my birth: York, Pennsylvania.

In my mid-20s, curiosity led me to dig in and begin the search into my true identity. I wanted to know what nationality and heritage I could claim. I could not answer any medical history questions at the doctor's office, I knew nothing. The first call I made was to the York County Hospital. The lady in charge of records insisted I could not gain access to my birth record without an attorney.

Without being too terribly discouraged, I called 411 Information and asked for any children's home agency in York. I was offered a listing. I called and spoke briefly to the receptionist as I told her about my quest to learn exactly where I came from. I was merely requesting any information I could be offered, if in fact I found the right place where my journey had begun years before.

After being placed on a short hold with elevator music, she returned to the line and happily stated she would be connecting me to the administrator; the actual woman who handled my adoption case. I couldn't believe my luck! With all the legalities of sealed birth records, she was only permitted to release non-identifying information. I was eager and thankful to hear anything and everything because the only other tangible piece of evidence I had to claim for myself was the date of my birth: October 9, 1969. She then proceeded to tell me what she could.

My mother was 15 years old when she gave birth to me and was the eldest of 9 children. Her own mother had recently passed away, so she was deemed responsible for her younger siblings and the upkeep of the household. Her father worked to support his brood. She was 5'8, weighed 140 pounds and had blonde hair and blue eyes. She was considered to be a wild child and hippie, labeled a drug addict and an alcoholic.

I was also informed of her diabetes. There was no information the woman could offer that related to my biological father. Perhaps he was drafted or enlisted to Vietnam by choice. He is a mystery too.

After bringing me into the world, my natural mother turned me over to foster care, then took me back, on three separate occasions. The third and final time, she relinquished me to The Children's Home of York and allowed me to be placed into a permanent foster home while going into the system to await eligible adoption. When this woman, who was my caseworker then, placed me with the people who were selected to adopt me, I am sure she had aspired for it to be a healthy decision. There was no way for her to foresee the lifetime of sadness I was about to endure. She was deeply troubled to hear my story.

I always knew I would write a book about my life. At many uncertain times, I never realized how beneficial the process would turn out to be. For many years I procrastinated for one reason or another, possibly afraid to reveal the bittersweet memories that did not know the innocence of childhood. My story is not an easy one to tell. As I am finally writing these words to you, I still feel a slight, loathsome dread as I face old wounds and lessons head on once again.

I truly hope you may draw upon my tribulations, challenges and hardships to help strengthen yourself to navigate the storms in your own life. An indomitable spirit will carry you far. At last, I am coming to the discovery of who I am, as I am now strong enough and brave enough to share my story.

RAINBOW IN THE DARK

The people who were selected to adopt me were Earl and Mabel, a middle aged couple. A child knows or can maybe just feel if things are not quite right. At such a young age, we have no other choice but to believe they are. Earl constantly ranted and raved, no matter what the issue. I watched him hurt Mabel by punching and kicking her while she did her best to deflect his blows and pleaded for him to stop. Her screams terrified me.

The only thing I could do was hide under my bed and listen. I was never safe but it felt like it was with the under bed heater vent warming and comforting me. There were many times he would drag me out from under that bed to hit and hurt me too.

One early winter morning, with darkness still outside, I felt so much anger towards him for what he did to her the night before. He told me to let the dog out. In my mother's defense I said, "Why should I?" As quickly as I had said the words, he turned to her, because he couldn't reach me and said, "Slap her!" Without any sort of warning, she slapped me hard across my face. I let the dog out with a heart crushed by betrayal. I was four.

We lived in a white mobile home that had a black stripe, far out into the country on a two-lane road not traveled very often. When I was five years old, I must have realized the way I was living was all wrong. I knew what a hobo-stick was and that I was to tie all of my valuable possessions into it. I knew I wanted to run away. As I was walking down the long driveway and nearing the road, I saw Earl running down the lawn after me.

Instead of gently taking my hand into his and explaining why what I was doing was so dangerous, he snatched me up by my arm then dragged me back up to the trailer, where he then proceeded to beat me excessively with his hands and belt until I had large welts from the buckle. I learned right then to resent Mabel even more, as she stood in the doorway and laughed at my shrieking screams of pain and terror. Again, I felt her betrayal and wondered why I ever cared about her.

Starting out with my first year of formal schooling after kindergarten, I was labeled as an outcast and there was usually a note attached to my report card which stated that I was a child who did not get along well with others. Before going to school, I never had friends or playmates but I did have cousins with whom I was permitted to stay over on the weekends. We would go rollerskating, then would huddle around the radio in the dark on Saturday nights while listening to spooky stories narrated by Vincent Price. They had a stable home where I saw and experienced how children were intended to be treated and I was always treated like one of them. My ugly home life world did not exist here next to the forest, even further out into the farmland and countryside.

From a very young age, I have vivid memories of my father touching me inappropriately. I can remember being as young as a toddler lying on the changing mat atop the washer. He would touch my vagina nearly every single day. By the age of three, I knew that it was wrong, not just instinctively. Supposedly sitting in the comfort of daddy's arms, I would repeatedly have to ask him to stop because it hurt. Around this time, I began to bite my nails to barely nubs and ripped my cuticles to see them bleed.

Right up until around the age of six, he would make me shower with him and put soap on his penis. I had no idea how corrupt what he was doing to me was, but even worse how sick it was- what he was making me do to him. I realized how wrong it all was when sleeping over at my cousins' home. At first, I thought it was a normal interaction between a father and daughter. When I learned that it wasn't from observing my relatives, I felt too confused and ashamed to ask or tell anyone.

Time passed by and I was growing older and wiser. I would stand up to my father and refuse to shower with him and touch him and he was not going to touch me ever again or I would tell anyone who would listen. Before this time, it began to make me feel physically sick when he would touch me. It always became a part of the night's agenda when Mabel would go bowling on Thursday nights.

It constantly got to the point of me getting into hysterics because I didn't want to be left alone with him. She ignored my pleas time and time again to take me with her. I resented her more by this time because her mental and physical abuse began to grow worse with severity. A few times she made me bleed and I had bruises that lasted for weeks from her beating me with whatever object was close at hand.

I learned to despise structured religion even though I was a part of the children's choir and was also an acolyte at the United Methodist Church. I could not understand how my father could socialize at church on Sunday's and act like a perfect saint, while during the rest of the week, he would portray absolute evil.
Many times Mabel wore dark sunglasses to church in an attempt to conceal her black eyes. I was thankful my random bruises were usually in not so obvious places. Every bruise though, carved a deeper scar within my soul.

Around age 9, I was beginning to get interested in the entire concept of beauty. I believed if I could make myself look pretty on the outside, I could erase the ugliness I felt on the inside from despair. When we would attend church, they were each in their Sunday school classes, and I was to be in mine but I never was. I would leave the church in defiance and would walk around the block to visit an old Native American man, Little Turtle, at his shop. I think he knew I was a troubled child. He would allow me to try on all of his beautiful sterling silver and turquoise jewelry while he told me fascinating stories about his Navajo heritage.

I then made my way to the drugstore across the street to steal candy then later make-up. I used to even steal money directly from the church offering plates. I hated the church and its congregation. I blamed their narrow minded ideals as a contributor to my fathers instability. He was the custodian for the church, and I watched them degrade and run him into the ground mentally, when all he wanted to do was a good job and to be appreciated and accepted, which he never was. In his entire life he always carried with him a black sheep mentality from his childhood and into his day-to-day existence.

In the summer of 1978, we moved into Camp Hill, a suburb of Harrisburg, PA. One afternoon Earl and I were on our way to pick Mabel up from work. In amazement, I saw miles of Grateful Dead followers, or Deadheads if you will, making their way to a concert on City Island. Around the same time while at the local Capital City Mall, I got to get in super close to the band KISS because I ducked under The KISS ARMY. Their costumes and makeup both scared and fascinated me at the same time.

The following autumn upon entering a new grade school, I already had a huge chip on my shoulder from home life and the transition of everything combined, proved to make my general attitude a little bit worse. My grades quickly went from C's and D's to eventually F's and a lot of I's for incomplete work. Repeating the grade was often threatened each school year. Comprehending the subjects, particularly with math, turned into a grueling task between the teachers and myself. No one has identified that I have dyslexia.

In school, I really was trying my hardest despite what I was being told. There was not one test that I ever passed, no matter how much studying I tried to do to prepare. It seemed as though I was getting into trouble for something or other constantly. I was quick to use profanity towards teachers that liked to humiliate me in front of the class because I didn't understand the lesson. Overall, my attitude continued to get darker, yet I still tried to maintain childlike views and aspirations.

Every Memorial Day, the town of Camp Hill would host a parade. My absolute favorite part of that parade was waiting for, then watching and admiring the girls from Beverly's Dance Academy. While making their way down the street, they performed tap and ballet dance routines. I so badly wanted to join them and wear the pretty little silk and sequined outfits that they got to wear. It felt like every little girl in town was granted permission and even encouraged to attend the classes, except for me. I begged Earl and Mabel to be able to participate. They refused my wish many times.

I joined the Girl Scouts and stayed happily involved with all the fun activities and new things to learn, based on skills for the badges on my sash. Each year, I sold Girl Scout cookies with a passion to pay for a week or two of summer camp. I went to Camp Small Valley, when it was still a horseback riding camp. It was here, where I learned about proper horse riding techniques, like posting and trotting. I loved to learn and gain knowledge about the necessary care of horses, like grooming and the general maintenance involved.

The horse I got to ride the most was 16 hands high and we were also permitted to raise the bar on the fence posts higher and higher in order to practice jumping. Flying through the air on such a magnificent beast was exhilarating. I loved to go out into the wilderness on camping trips to learn all the wonders of living out under the stars along with basic survival skills, in case I ever found myself stranded alone in the woods, lost.

I was at a Girl Scout meeting on March 30, 1981. As we sat around the tables working on craft projects, while listening to the radio, we learned that President Reagan had nearly been assassinated. It was hard to believe that something so horrible could happen. That very same meeting, after all the other girls in the troop had been picked up, I was beginning to wonder why I hadn't been. I continued working on my craft project while the leaders cleaned up.

Mabel finally arrived and I could see that she had been crying and she looked very upset and frantic as she spoke to one of the women in charge. They were both looking at me with concern, but I didn't know what they were saying because I was on the other side of the hall. I could tell by the way they were looking at me that something was wrong. after calling me over, they both carefully explained to me that Earl attempted to take his own life. I would have to go home with the troop leader for dinner and the evening while Mabel returned to the hospital until Earl's condition was stabilized.

Again, I felt shame that he valued my quality-of-life so little, never mind his own, that he would choose suicide to cope with his problems. No matter how I looked at it: his problems were my problems. My father continued to lapse deeper into mental illness as time went on. He began consuming whiskey and beer and when mixed with his medications, the effects of intoxication were even more apparent. Many times, I would just stare at him in repulsion at his state of inebriation, along with the sickening comments he still continued to make to me.

During the course of trying to figure out what exactly was going on in my life through multiple counseling sessions, I had to see the doctor for bad headaches. I told him my parents hit and hurt me. He looked at them and told them to not hit me on my head anymore. It felt like he was saying that hitting me everywhere else was ok. I learned the term manic depression for my father along the way.

BIG BALLS

I began smoking cigarettes on a regular basis around age ten by merely presenting a coupon from the Sunday paper which entitled the bearer to a free pack of the newest brand. I had a newspaper route so I nabbed all the cigarette coupons from my patrons' papers.

Otherwise, you only needed a note from an adult which would ask the store clerk to please allow you to purchase their smokes. Those notes were easy to forge.

Marlboro Reds became my brand of choice to match the tough girl image I was trying to uphold. If I couldn't fit in, I was going to stand out.

The days of my cutting classes were accumulating fast. The truant officer was constantly on my heels. To avoid him, I began to stay near the woods and other concealed areas to get wherever it was that I was going.

I continued to find creative ways to steal and shoplift. I could spend hours in the mall or other stores without a dime while filling my backpack. I didn't need half of what I had ripped off, but it was a game. I loved the sport of the hunt while I was being hunted.

When I entered the small town high school in the seventh grade, I had an entirely bad outlook on life which was filled with anger and hate toward everything my life consisted of. I didn't care about anything or anyone. I carried that disposition with me everywhere.

When I would return home after a supposed day of education, I went directly up the stairs to my room, which were two feet inside the front door without any sort of small talk.

I would then put on one of my heavy metal records, which they hated, and would crank my stereo as loud as it would go while I sat smoking out of my bedroom window.

I had already begun sneaking around at night by climbing out onto the porch roof outside of my bedroom window and then would jump off. I had to be careful to not land the wrong way, but like a cat I was a night prowler and usually landed on my feet. I later convinced them to give me an actual key for after school.

Little did they know, I was hardly ever in school and I only wanted the key to come and go as I pleased during the day or night. When I was missing in action, I didn't have to answer to anyone. I began running away for days and weeks at a time because I couldn't take life as it was any longer.

I came home from school one afternoon and found the house and especially the kitchen in complete shambles. There were shards of broken glass everywhere from two liquor bottles. It was a disgusting mess. Upon entering a little further, I passed the kitchen and into the living room where I found Earl slumped over in his recliner with blood all over him, with cuts to his wrists once again. That was my childhood breaking point. I hated my life and I knew I had to make a change. He was once again checked into a mental health facility.

I began to hang out primarily with the druggies or the Heads, as they were known. Most of the guys wore black, leather jackets, concert T-shirts and had long, unruly hair.

The majority of the school was overrun by the Preppies. They consisted primarily of the upper middle-class and upper class of our small town. They were the ones who wore a polo shirt faithfully every day with the alligator and had their collar flipped up with penny loafers or Docksiders. Not my style.

My daily attire was a Leather or Levi's jeans jacket with Levi's jeans and a hoodie. Combat or black boots, a T-shirt underneath and a bandanna tied gypsy-style on my head.

The Heads did not conform to the social pressures of high school. We were the kids standing across the street, smoking cigarettes and weed during the lunch break and always debated returning inside after. If we did get through the day, our after school activities usually always included sitting in someone's black light lit up bedroom listening to Black Sabbath or Rush in weed smoke so thick you could hardly see the person across from you.

After years of personal torture from not fitting in because I was not provided the designer Jordache and Bon Jour jeans all the other kids were wearing, combined with being made fun of for being adopted, after awhile I didn't want to fit in anymore. I grew a deeper resentment toward the entire structure of school but particularly towards teachers and the classes they taught that I was failing miserably. Now it was definitely my fault.

For a while, I was trying so hard to study for tests and even do my homework on rare occasions. It still hurt deep down that I just wasn't understanding the subjects, no matter how hard I tried. I failed science class flat-out because I refused to dissect a fat frog.

Trying and failing felt a lot worse than not doing any of it and getting into trouble or upset which I was used to anyway. I would attempt to reach out for help with assignments at home and I struggled along the best I could until I finally gave up.

What I needed to learn would be gained through worldly knowledge, not in a classroom setting. I knew I was more than capable of teaching myself academics.I had a desire to learn, though I found myself sitting in detention most afternoons.

I had two friends that both lived on the wealthiest, old money side of town. One friend lived in a house as big as a mansion. Her living area was the entire third floor. The three of us experimented with each other and mostly practiced kissing.

I did carry subtle feelings of guilt, though not nearly as intense as when Mabel caught me masturbating and proceeded to tell me what a dirty girl

I was. It was even more demented when she would demand to smell my fingers at her urging to detect if I had been playing with myself recently. It was very degrading.

I never heard of other parents resorting to such twisted measures. She even went as far to tell me that my feet, which were black from running barefoot all day, were cleaner than my vile vagina. It made me have a very negative view of myself, my sexuality and sex in general.

Those events led me to become more inquisitive and curious about sex in general, so I often looked through Earl's top dresser drawer which was filled with all types of porn. Books, magazines, movies- you name it. I learned a lot through all that literature, but it did make me feel creepy because they belonged to him.

He was still behaving in a predatory way at times and would purposely sit in an area or spot where he could get a direct line of sight to watch me exit the bathroom after a shower or bath. He would still make nasty comments and would work himself up to the point of violence. He continued to blame me for his behavior and made me believe it was me that provoked it. It wasn't my fault but many times I believed it was.

Both parents continued to take a plethora of medications for uses ranging from depression and anxiety to painkillers. Earl was diagnosed with Non-Hodgkin's Lymphoma so he had a small pharmacy. Mabel took Ativan daily for her bad nerves.

Before I reached my final breaking point, one afternoon at eleven years old, I took an overdose of 21 Ativan. I did not want to die, I merely wanted to escape my personal hell for a while. I was in and out of consciousness for nearly 2 days. I was laying on the fold out couch bed just inside the front door. At some point they would've had to check the mail. Too busy to notice an unconscious child?

On the second day, I regained enough awareness to call 911. Before the paramedics arrived, I lost consciousness again. I woke up in a pediatric emergency department while vomiting from Syrup of Ipecac, until every last bit of the medication was out of my system.

I requested to see Earl to tell him that I finally understood his desperation in being led to wanting to end his own life. He refused to come and see me. I hated him more than ever.

METAL HEALTH

One day, Earl was beating Mabel up in the kitchen. I screamed at him to stop and in the flash of a second, all of his rage, hostility and anger were directed towards me. He lunged to grab me and had I not been quick to jump backwards, he would've landed completely on top of me. That only made him even more mad. I kept looking behind me as I ran up the stairs to my bedroom.

As I hurried in, I locked the door and attempted to block it behind me. I thought he might just leave me alone. Within a minute, I heard his heavy footsteps stomping up the staircase – then silence – then he plowed himself through my door.

He threw me violently around the room while swinging his balled up fists, as I did my best to defend myself. I was able to get past him and ran across the street to an elderly couple's home with Mabel and for the first time I made her call the police. When they arrived, she refused to file a report. It was at that moment I told her that I was not going to be subjected to her or his insane behavior anymore – if he or she was not willing to change it. I vowed I would leave and never come back.

It was that day when I realized I had to do something drastic to escape the life I was trapped in. I was searching for order in my life and I was determined to find it. After several more bouts of running away and hiding around my town, I grew tired of it all and eventually refused to return to school and furthermore, refused to return home. The local chief-of-police already knew me well. I called him one evening and asked him to come and pick me up at my location.

I explained the entire situation to him as I sat in his office. This time was so different from the past when I usually had to sit there while he gave me long-winded lectures relating to how I would never amount to anything while reveling in juvenile delinquency. This time as I was talking, he looked at me somewhat puzzled and listened intently as I made my official request.

I asked him to call Cumberland County Children and Youth Services to find a placement for me. If he didn't, he would continue to be on the lookout for me and hauling me in. We were both tired of that game.

He asked if I was absolutely sure this is what I wanted. Once the wheels were set in motion, there would be no turning back. The only thing I was sure of was that I did not want, in any further situations with Earl and Mabel to cry or be hurt in any way, any more. I really wanted to believe that maybe just maybe there was a chance for me to be placed into a normal home and feel like a normal child. I wanted to believe that somehow there had been a horrible mistake – the wrong couple had been allowed to adopt me. By placing myself back into the system, I thought I had a chance to be genuinely loved by people who actually wanted me.

The chief escorted us to the break room, when he let me know that a representative from Children and Youth Services was on their way from Carlisle to come get me. We sat there and talked some more while drinking Cokes and eating vending machine snacks while we waited. At last, a woman came and I was on my way to a new life. When we got to the building, I sat briefly in the waiting room with mothers and children of all ages. It was loud and all a bit overwhelming.

They did allow me to smoke so I kept stepping outside into the rain and cold while I waited to be introduced to my caseworker. I was eventually called back through a long hallway with offices on either side. The hallway was dark for some reason. A very full-figured black woman stepped out of her office while extending her hand. She was very nice and introduced herself while explaining what her role was and what I should expect while many questions were asked as to why I found myself sitting across from her.

We walked together up the block to the Cumberland County Courthouse. I had to appear in front of a judge to be officially placed into the foster care system. My caseworker stated she would be seeking a permanent placement for me but in the meantime, she found a temporary foster family for me to stay with. Being 11, meant it was a little more challenging to find a permanent placement that wanted an older child. It was the foster mother who came to get me.

She brought along with her another foster child, a girl around my age. The couple had two other foster kids besides her. It seemed all nice and pleasant at first because everything was a brand new world. In only a few days, I knew that it wasn't normal. The dad constantly groped me and tried to fondle me, while pulling me onto his lap. It didn't take long to see he was messing with the others too.

The mom went into town to shop, so us kids were left alone. I thought I was confiding in the girl closest to my age and I thought we were going to agree that what he was doing was wrong. She not only accepted it as normal behavior, she defended him to the point of attacking me when I threatened to tell. She beat me up pretty bad. My short lived dream of a happy home with a white picket fence went out the window fast.

When the mother returned home, I had my belongings packed and demanded to be returned to Children and Youth Services. On the way, she kept repeatedly asking me what had happened while she was gone. Feeling so disgusted and angry, I couldn't even speak because I couldn't believe how ridiculous fate could be. After several hours of waiting in the lobby, I was placed into another foster home for the night with an older couple.

The next morning, I was back in my caseworker's office. I don't know why but I refused to mutter a single word and reveal the real reason for my dislike of the first placement. It felt as if talking about it directly would confirm that I am only worth this type of treatment, particularly from adult men. She let me know she had a great placement in mind for me: She was happy. I was happy.

The couple were in their late 20s and were unable to conceive and bear children on their own. After years of failed fertility treatments, they opened their home and hearts to foster children. Placed with them already, was a one and two-year-old brother and sister. I would be their first adolescent. Were they ready for me? Probably not.

I had to wait nearly the entire day by entertaining myself with walks, while I waited for the father to pick me up after his workday was done. It was dark and dinner had long since been prepared and served at their home, so we went across the street to Hamilton's restaurant. That was an awkward dinner. Here was this nice man who was naïve and unsuspecting of who I was becoming. He bought me ice cream for dessert, so I let my tough girl persona rest a bit.

As he was driving us to their home, the scenery left the lights of town behind and we headed out into the country. The stars and moonlight piqued my curiosity about everything even more. We made the turn onto their road and to the left and right were peach orchards before the dirt road driveway continued to wind back through the woods. As we were nearing their home, he explained to me that they had just completed building it a few years before. There were several areas not yet complete, such as the basement swimming pool.

I had him pretty well down, now I just wanted to reach their home over the river and through the woods to meet her and my little foster siblings. Upon our arrival, she met us on the front porch with the baby girl on her hip and the boy hiding behind her legs, peeking out. After initial introductions, she gave me a tour of their house which included being shown to my room. The pretty little blue flowers on the walls were homey but the problem was my room was on the side of the house that was not yet complete and a framing wall was blocking what would've been a window.

The rest of the house was all state of the art beautiful, resembling a home you would see in a major architecture design magazine. I did like my room. As I was unpacking and getting my things put away in the closet and dresser drawers, she popped her head in the door and asked if there was anything that I needed. I asked her for a clock radio. My little space was now complete.

As I drifted off to sleep that night I remember the anticipation I felt as I looked forward to the morning to come so I could see and discover exactly where I was.

WE'RE NOT GONNA TAKE IT

A few weeks into my placement with them, I was given a JCPenney and Sears Wish Book catalog and was asked to pick out some outfits – anything and everything I liked. At Christmas, I received every last thing on my list. That was very nice and very unexpected.

Every Sunday morning, we went to church as a family. Sunday afternoon would always include lunch and a very long visit at the grandparents house for the afternoon.

One particular Sunday, while they were all in the other room cooing over the babies, I was growing bored feeding pennies into a bubblegum machine that gave you cashews. As I sat there, I began to look around. Above me was a very large collection of tiny liquor bottles lined up on a high shelf which went around all four walls.

There was a lot of liquor from all over the world. The tiny bottles were placed so close together, with duplicates of some, the temptation grew too strong to resist to not take a few. None would be easily missed. I opened a bottle and downed a giant gulp of gin and did my best to keep it down and then scrambled to conceal the smell of booze on my breath. I gathered a nice collection in my purse and coat pockets by the time we were ready to leave.

The fancy clothing could not conceal the rebellious, defiant, adventurous girl I was at heart. I would steal multiple packs of cigarettes, especially from the grocery store on the weekly shopping trip. Whenever I could get my hands on them, they were nabbed. All stores made them easily accessible for sticky fingers like mine. I was very adamant about maintaining my vices.

While they thought I was down at the pond ice-skating every afternoon, I was actually sitting on the far side of a huge dirt mound on the edge of the forest, sipping and taste testing different liquor while smoking my cigarettes. I had a lot to contemplate once again.

With this placement, there was another form of weirdness I was forced to deal with. I really didn't know how to deal with it. My foster father and mother walked around nude all the time. I remember hearing them give me all kinds of reasonings but none made sense to me.

What freaked me out even more is when they started trying to encourage me to walk around nude as well. I refused that aspect of the scenario and pretty much told them it made me feel uncomfortable all the way around.

I had just turned 12 and I was beginning to develop breasts so I wanted to keep my body under my clothes and all to myself. It was just a weird situation. I resorted to my vices to cope.

I was enrolled in the local middle school earlier in the year. I was still attempting to complete the seventh grade. I had already failed once. I think I was disgusted and growing bored with life in general and ready to move on for different reasons.

I had a boyfriend named Forest. He was a grade ahead of me. One night, after making our plans, I snuck out of the house then walked through the spooky moonlit woods out to the main road where I waited for him.

He was able to take his grandmother's car because she was always fast asleep at this time of night. As I waited there on the side of the road, I wasn't sure if he was going to come or not but then there were headlights and it was him!

We went back to his trailer so he didn't get caught with the car and as we were making our way through the hallway in the dark to his bedroom, his grandmother opened the door and saw me.

She gave Forest a strange look but then closed the door again. We sat there after turning the space heater on and smoked a joint or two along with a beer, then laid down beside each other and fell asleep.

When I woke up he was not beside me, he was out in the kitchen with his grandmother. Just as I was reaching the kitchen, he looked up at me and said, "I'm sorry." Just as he was saying the words- came the knock at the door- you know, a cop knock. They picked me up and hauled me back out to the foster home. Traitor.

I was vulnerable to sexuality as a whole and so far the various bad experiences were starting to get to me. Since my encounters had not been normal, perhaps I was a little too sensitive. No, it was all getting more uncomfortable by the day. When the father mentioned corporal punishment to address something I had done that was unacceptable, that was it for me. I called him a sick freak because I was almost a teenager. That was the exact moment I knew I wanted to move on.

I decided to take two of my little whiskey bottles to school. I had already been buying white cross speeders regularly, along with Valiums and I wanted to see how they mixed. Upon entering the girls room first thing that morning in a hurry, I plopped my backpack onto one of the sinks. Just as I was getting into a stall, I heard the crash. I ran out and could see the backpack landed with the pocket side down which held the bottles and one of them was broken.

The entire bathroom was filled with the smell of bourbon. I think I was panicking, so I mopped it up the best I could with paper towels after I got the glass removed. I was definitely late for the first period, so I rushed to my locker, threw the backpack inside and then headed off to class. I had pills on the top shelf of my locker and didn't bother to put them away. About three class periods later, the principal pulled me out of class personally.

As I exited the classroom, to the left of the doorway was a police officer. I asked him if he was going to arrest me. He told me to watch my smart mouth. As we made our way through the school to the front where the offices were, the kids we passed in the hall were dumbstruck having never before seen a student being escorted by a police officer with the principal. When we reached his office, the principal sat me down and then proceeded to inform me that because of my prior offenses which had already resulted in two in school and one out of school suspension, I was now being expelled. His school would not tolerate such antics of a delinquent.

I was driven to Children and Youth Services with all of my belongings in complete silence with the foster father. I went inside and met with my caseworker after he dropped me off. Again, I did not mention the corrupt nude advocates and my true feelings of the situation, I just took the blame for it all not working. I had to appear in front of the judge again, though this time he was not nice to me at all. He gave me the label of incorrigible, which means cannot be corrected with no hope for reform. He was not happy with me in the least and even threatened to put me into a juvenile detention facility if I did not straighten up.

I was placed into another temporary foster home. The poor old man walked me through their home to my bedroom and closed the door. Within five minutes of entering their home, I jumped out of my second-story bedroom window to my freedom. I was later picked up by the police then driven to yet another foster home. All the while I was falling farther and farther behind in the inevitable dooming school year. It was nice to be out legally and I didn't have to hear the guilt trip about how far behind I was.

ROUND AND ROUND

A few days passed by before my caseworker came to the house and told me to gather my things – she would explain what was happening in the car. Children and Youth Services had come to the conclusion and decision that it would be more suitable for me to be in a more structured environment. I was being placed in an actual children's home, the Children's Aid Society in Chambersburg which housed girls and boys that could not manage to fit into other placements like me.

When we got there, some kids were in the large kitchen with an adult overseeing their tasks. On the other side of the great room were hallways with rooms; boys on the right, girls on the left. Surrounding the main gathering area were small rooms used for different purposes such as visits or as I later learned, one of the rooms was used for punishment. The director reminded me of an alien and she wore very stinky perfume. It was so heavy you could taste it, paired along with hideous blue eyeshadow on her lids. It was a lot for my senses.

She then went on to detail exactly what was expected of me while I was residing at the children's home. First, every resident had designated days for meal preparation and cleanup after each meal. This cleanup included the dining hall and to complete kitchen chores like scrubbing pots and pans. There was a daily routine to be followed and everyone pretty much knew what they were doing and when they were to be doing it. There was also a Level system in which you could earn privileges.

If you behaved, went to school and followed each and every rule, you could advance through the Levels. In due time, you could advance to Level Four, which gave you the most freedom to walk downtown on your own or to go see a movie on the weekends. A full, unsupervised night out on the town. Smoking was permitted if you had the means to purchase your own cigarettes. Your family could send care packages or bring cartons on visit days.

I did get enrolled in the local middle school and for a while was trying to act right. Earl and Mabel were encouraged to visit. The realization eventually came that no matter how good I was, no matter how bad I wanted to go back to familiar territory, I was sick of the system already and had nowhere to go. I also realized Earl was never going to do his part to get himself mentally stable and well. He refused to participate in any form of therapy.

Subjecting myself to the insanity of abuse and still never knowing what was going to happen next would be a certain reality if I was to return home. It felt like a cruel joke of sorts. I began to resent their visits and eventually told them not to come visit me anymore.
My roommate was a chronic runaway like me. After spending a short time together, we began to plan our first getaway.

The windows of the building were easy to pop the screen out after you cranked the glass window open.
Most of the entire living layout of the building was on one floor so we could easily jump out with ease; and did so many times. The first few excursions we only went downtown to hang out with kids our age and smoked weed. The old fashioned lamp posts that lined the streets gave off a warm glow. It was fun and exciting at first. Eventually, the cops had our descriptions down and we were constantly getting picked up.

After getting tired of being apprehended every which way we moved, we made our way down toward the beaches of Delaware, yet somehow we ended up in Baltimore, Maryland. Before entering the system, Earl and Mabel went to Rehoboth Beach every year. Earl took me to the boardwalk one year to buy a T-shirt. I ended up getting a mint colored spaghetti strap top but he wouldn't let me get the decal I wanted. He insisted I get the decal that read, "Flat is Beautiful"

We wandered through the streets feeling very out of place. We found ourselves smack dab in the middle of the red light district. There were many bars and clubs that lined the streets with neon signs, as well as scantily dressed women standing just outside the doors trying to lure customers in. As we sat for a few hours on the curb, we watched the flurry of activity going on around us while trying our hardest not to stand out. We were wedged in between two parked cars.

We had arrived earlier in the day, after walking around forever it seemed. We experimented with asking for money as we tried to figure out what we were going to do. We were near exhaustion. All the tourists of Inner Harbor seemed to look at us with disgust instead of pity. We sat in between those parked cars until after dark. I don't remember what we were contemplating but I do remember feeling very lost, never mind completely out of place.

Someone warned us to be careful because the local police were adamant about picking up derelicts, vagrants and runaways off the streets. The reason being we were told was that such walks of life gave the city a bad image. We were close to the waterfront and there was a definite chill in the air so we decided to stay awake for the night, continuously walking around to keep warm. During the day we would find a safe place to crash. We were two young girls and it was obvious to us that we had to get out of this part of town before some pimp or otherwise might try to steal and recruit us.

The first few months I was out on the streets, I lost 40 pounds by being hungry all the time. We often walked for miles with our thumbs out trying to catch a ride. I was learning how to like and appreciate my body, now that I had a shape and breasts. I didn't feel like the ugly duckling anymore.

There were all kinds of bars and dance clubs with people lingering outside; some were waiting to get in,while others were saying their goodbyes. As we walked down the streets, each establishment was blaring its own style of music. Couples were dressed to the nines and were coming out arm in arm out of candlelit restaurants. They waited in the crisp night air while a valet brought their car.

The aroma of food only made us hungry, or hungrier than we already were. I learned early on how to fill up on water. The nice restaurants and bars at least gave you ice in the water to give you the satisfaction of chewing something. We walked up and down each and every street, lingering as we went to take it all in. We were definitely not watching the time and how late it was getting while we strolled and pretended to have parents waiting for us back at some fancy hotel. It could've been the truth.

The only thing missing was money. We accumulated a few dollars between us, and earlier in the day we stashed all of our bags, which held all of our worldly possessions. We came upon a storefront that had a bright neon blue sign hung in the large bay window which read: Gypsy Tarot and Palm Readings by a gifted psychic. Long heavy curtains were parted in the center. Intrigued, we stood up in the doorway and tried to catch a glimpse of a real, live gypsy or witch. There was a crystal ball sitting on the center of the table.

We stood there for a few minutes talking and discussing our plans, when a lady opened the door and looked at us without leaving her doorway. She did not look like the fortuneteller I had conjured up in my mind, she was very pretty. She then asked if we would like to know what the future had in store for us. I was the only one who wanted to get a reading. I told her I did not have any money so maybe next time. The fortuneteller invited us to come inside. She was willing to perform a reading for me free of charge because business had been slow anyway that day.

I was amazed by the reading and her accuracy however, at the end of our session she made an uncanny prediction. She stated I would encounter trouble soon but I would be able to escape an unsatisfactory situation. With those final ominous words, my reading was over and we left. We were walking and talking, again not paying much attention to what was going on around us. We looked up for a moment at a stoplight and noticed a cop standing on the corner.

It was too late to turn around and head back in the opposite direction. The deer in the headlights image comes to mind. We stood there calmly on that corner, with the cop waiting for the light to change so we could cross the street. In those few short minutes, something definitely did not add up to the cop. Two teenage girls, alone on the streets late at night. That was it-we were snagged.

He began to question us, then wasted no time taking us to the police station and handcuffing us to a long wooden bench. We refused to mutter a single word. After the standoff that continued on to dawn, we were released and my cohort decided to give herself up to Children and Youth Services and was returned to Pennsylvania. I was determined to make it to the beach. I had to walk for a while before a car finally pulled over. I decided to go for real to Ocean City, Maryland. No particular reason, other than it seemed like a fun place to go.

When I arrived, it was a full moon night. My ride dropped me off on the strip so I could see what the town had to offer. I was enthralled and full of life, without a care in the world. I hopped into a T-Top Trans Am and sat in the backseat, looking up at the moon with the ocean air cooling my skin as my hair got all messed up from the wind. I didn't care. I felt beautiful and free.

One of the guys told me his parents were gone for the evening so I could come out to his house and party then crash in their travel trailer, after we hung out for a while. His family owned a farm where chickens were raised for market. From the moment we first pulled into the driveway, the stench of ammonia from chicken urine was overly strong. I could see their cornfield to our right as we were heading toward his house. The next morning, he came out to the camper and told me his parents knew that I was there and his mother had prepared a big breakfast.

I was welcome to come in and if I needed to, I could shower and sleep in the spare bedroom that night and could do work on their farm for some cash for a few days. The offer sounded great. As soon as I walked through the kitchen screen door, his father began studying me closely while peering at me over his newspaper. He asked how old I was. I confirmed 17.

He kept asking me questions such as if my parents knew where I was and such. He knew I was a runaway but didn't let on right away. He still obliged me to work, cleaning the chicken coops for a small pittance. That is a smell you never forget. That night I got to shower and sleep in a real bed in a comfy nightgown while my clothes were being washed.

28

As I looked at myself in the mirror, I was still getting used to my new image. Before I arrived in Ocean City, I was dropped off at some out of the way town. I went into a store to steal some Sun-In and a few bottles of peroxide. After having brown hair most of my life, I was now a blonde. I also attempted to cut my own hair, so it was probably apparent I was trying to alter my appearance.

The next morning at breakfast, the dad was still overly inquisitive as to who I really was and where I came from. I exploded on him and assured him I would gladly move on. He simmered down, at the urging of his wife, so my new friend and I headed to the beach for the day to play in the sunshine. When we returned to the farmhouse, there were three police cars parked in the driveway. Before we even got close to their house, I jumped out of the car and ran into the cornfields, zigzagging as fast as I could go.

I was not going to give up without a fight. I kept going until I felt concealed. A cop got on his bull horn and was trying to command me to come out. No way! I did not move. I remained hidden until I heard the very last cop car heading to the main road. When I emerged, my friend and his father were talking near his car.

The father began to speak to me. He knew that I was only 13 and a runaway. He and his family were not going to be jeopardized any further by harboring me. I shouted back at him and demanded he give me a ride. I assured him I didn't want to be in their hair anymore either. As the father was driving me into town, he divulged that he had someone he wanted me to meet.

I thought that was code for taking me to jail. He then promised that after the visit he would take me to the bus station and buy a ticket for me to wherever I wanted to go. Sounded fair enough. We pulled up to a high-rise building. At that time, I did not know they were called condominiums. We took an elevator all the way up to the 18th floor.

We were then standing at a door with PH on it. He knocked, then a beautiful woman answered the door and invited us in. After she served us cold drinks, we sat there on the couch as I was asking myself why in fact this man had brought me here. We all sat and talked for a bit before she stated the reason for our meeting. She told me to get up and take a walk around her home.

I stepped out onto the terrace overlooking the Atlantic Ocean and took it all in while they continued to catch up inside. I then went back in and sat down across from her. I saw that she was holding an 8 x10 black and white photo. She told me to look at the girl and tell her what I saw. I held back the foremost and obvious descriptions: the girl's hair was matted and dirty and she looked run down with large black circles under her eyes. She looked a mess.

The lady revealed to me that the girl in the picture was her 22 years before when she herself was a runaway, turned junkie of heroin. I was shocked. She went on to remind me if I didn't change the path I was on, I could very well end up looking like the girl in the photo, or worse yet dead.

I had to ask how she managed to live and look like a movie star. She then told me the story of meeting the love of her life who changed her life for the better after meeting at a Narcotics Anonymous meeting 15 years before. He had just recently died and left her everything. I cannot remember my chosen destination for the bus ticket but I do remember getting on that bus feeling like I had been given a precious gift.

GYPSY ROAD

I was picked up by the cops somewhere along the way and returned like a criminal to the children's home. It didn't take long to understand that if I stayed anywhere in the surrounding tri-state area around Pennsylvania, New York and New Jersey, I would get picked up every time. I was in many foster homes across the central state. I would always end up at the police station. The cops learned they needed to handcuff me to something because I would be walked through the front door, sat down and left unattended. I would then merely get up and walk straight out the back door.

It was a drag being picked up a few states away though. Since I always ended up slipping through their fingers, they did begin to handcuff me to all kinds of things. It was a cat and mouse game. I would run. They would chase.

I was not affected by being brought back or being demoted to a lower level at the home. This would usually work for most kids. For me, the staff had to get creative with my particular punishment. I was made to live in one of those small rooms off of the great room. I was only permitted to wear my nightgown/pajamas 24 hours a day.

I think it was meant to be degrading, but I took it as notoriety within the home. I also think of the desperation they must have had because they didn't know what to do with me. I was an outcast rebel, and a flight-risk child. A local news reporter came to interview us, as wards of the state. I remember telling her my best friend was Jack Daniels.

The few most recent times the cops brought me back, I would be sure to give the kids a good show by kicking, screaming and biting the cops. I liked to act like I was delusional on drugs and alcohol. I was not nearly as impaired by a substance, only a little. I was only messed up on life.

So there I was, living in a little 12 x 12 room in my nightclothes. I had no problem getting my meal tray after all the other kids had sat down while striding past them all, making a joke of it. There were counselors that would have to come and sit and guard me. The door was left open with a couch sitting crosswise in front of it where they sat reading magazines, talking, guarding and watching me.

One Sunday afternoon, there were some sort of outing plans for all the kids; everyone except me.
There was an elderly on-call couple who were called in to keep an eye on me because all the regular counselors and other on-call workers were at the event. With everyone gone, it was just them and me. The woman smoked Salem cigarettes, so I pleaded with her to let me smoke a few since there was no way she could get into trouble. No cigarettes was also part of my punishment.

She and her husband were almost 70. Let the truth be known: I had already concocted an elaborate scheme for the ultimate breakout. I was just waiting to get back to my room to gather my clothes, instead of my night clothes which I was meant to be getting. I went to the closet for the woman to dispense my shampoo into a little paper cup as I gathered other hygiene things. She went back up front and her husband was perched midway down the hallway on the bench. He instructed me to go to my room, which I did to gather my clothes and most importantly, shoes.

I also filled a small bag to stash everything in. I slipped past him and closed the bathroom door behind me. I then turned the shower on to muffle the sound of me getting dressed and taking the window screen out. I wasn't actually completely dressed when the old woman began to open the door as I was already halfway out the window. I thought I grabbed everything from the shower stall but somehow, some damn way, I did not have my jeans.

I had a T-shirt, panties and shoes on as I was running like hell down the giant hill below the home. As cars were passing by I was shouting at them to stop gawking at me, I was wearing a bikini! I must've been quite a sight though, running full blast in my underwear and t-shirt. I got to the bottom of the hill and was getting pretty winded, with a huge cramp forming in my side, when I first heard the sirens. I was astonished at how the hunt had commenced so quickly. I was a fox being chased by dogs.

They were everywhere and all around me. At first, I figured I had a greater chance for successful avoidance if I could just rest for a few moments. No matter how fast I wanted to go it just wasn't happening anymore so I crouched down under a bush in someone's backyard to catch my breath and get the side-splitter to go away. After a short time, I didn't hear any further activity so I gave up my hiding place and started running again. I immediately heard men shout, "There she is!"

Several of the extra on-call workers that were at the event had been notified and summoned for back up along with the local slew of cops. It was all over but the fight was still going strong within. A very large cop tackled me and we wrestled around for a minute before I was completely restrained. As I stood up with assistance, another cop took off his coat and put it around me then zipped it up and told me to cover myself. The next few days at the home were quiet but I knew my days of continuing to reside there were numbered.

Sure enough, the caseworker from Children and Youth Services came to pick me up. She told me on the way that I was headed to a drug rehab. According to the powers that be, there was no way I could behave the way I did without being under the influence of drugs or alcohol. They had no idea how much of everything I felt was affecting me. Anger, hostility and overall hatred for the world.

My caseworker and I arrived at Clear Brook Lodge which was set way back on a long, wooded road. It looked like a peaceful place, being surrounded by the beautiful colors of autumn leaves. I was a bit nervous, and was assured that it was perfectly normal. I stalled a bit, smoking one cigarette after another. After one more Coke, I got up the nerve to go in and be asked 100 different questions by the intake counselor to dig deeper into who I really was. I would be expected to attend at least one group meeting a day, and follow a regimen of treatment sessions along with groups. We were all juveniles under 18; I was about to turn 14.

We filled our free time by telling our stories to each other, which made us feel closer as we walked along the football field to get as far away from the rehab as we could. Something began happening to me. Maybe it was hearing the war stories of real addicts that sobered my reality. Once a week, we would go into town to attend a meeting at the adult Clearbrook Manor. Hearing their stories invoked absolute fear.

As we become more adapted in our adult skin, we learn to create new forms of sabotage.

Once you have been walking down the wrong road for too long, it makes it even harder to turn back around and find a new road. I felt blessed in a way because so far I had managed to avoid such destructive temptations. Sitting and hearing all the heart wrenching stories, I realized that if I was not careful, I could easily end up where these people were.

Earl and Mabel came to visit with much needed cigarettes and money for the canteen. We took a few pictures and genuinely enjoyed the time we spent together. As the day of my release was approaching, I began to contemplate being good. I wanted to be on the straight and narrow path and I was willing to walk the line. I didn't want to be labeled a problem child anymore so I would do whatever was required of me while I was here and after I would apply myself and attend school every day.

My birthday finally came. I was 14 at last. With all the thoughts of straightening up my act, I couldn't help but feel more mature. You could even say I had become a young lady. In 28 days, I went from a child to a young adult. I was ready to graduate from the treatment program and start my new life.

I would be a responsible human being, in charge of guiding my own ship, instead of letting the winds blow my judgment around. The day before my release, I could not have been more serene. I thought for sure since I had made such positive progress, Children and Youth Services would find a nice home for me so I could get settled and get on with my life.

When the caseworker arrived, my eyes were red and swollen from crying because of tearful goodbyes with my treatment companions.

HEAVEN'S ON FIRE

It was nice to be on our way. At first, I had no idea where I was on my way to. I still had a vision in my mind of living in a nice foster home and being happy ever after. I was confident that I could be the good girl I had learned how to be. After a bathroom break, when I returned to the car she told me where I was going: Lourdesmont. The name itself created a lot of unpleasant images. She confirmed it was a combination between a private school and reformatory for wayward girls. It was run and operated by nuns.

I asked her, "Are you crazy?" I really felt like jumping out of the car at a stoplight as we were going through Clarks Summit, as I had done so many times before. Lourdesmont was out in the country about 5 miles or so. I knew this was not a good thing. All of my delusions came crashing into reality when we pulled into the driveway of the school. It looked very foreboding, like dark clouds should be hovering above it.

I knew I was not going to do well here. This cannot be happening. I said I would be good- not an angel.
Was it their mission to convert bad girls to convent? I was struggling with authority anyway and now they were expecting me to be governed by women who were married to God. I was already pissed at God; I didn't want to have to pretend to like his advocates.

My very first daydream vision, while I was sitting there , consisted of the scene from the Blues Brothers when they were getting whacked back-and-forth with a ruler by a nun when they said something wrong or filthy. I had to search for comedy. My caseworker tried to make me feel better by telling me to look at the other kids who seemed to be happy and that I should try to give it a fair chance. We sat together on what looked like a long church pew while we waited to speak to the mother superior or whatever they called her.

Again, I was compelled to run right out the door I came in. It was all over as far as I was concerned. After our meeting, my caseworker was sent on her way and I was left alone in the scholastic nightmare. A woman came and took me around the building and grounds for a tour. I was instructed to leave my bags in the office. There were 4 floors with a basement. The ground and second-floor consisted of the main school, which catered to all grades. The third and fourth floors were dorms for the girls who were to be reformed.

The rest of the students would come in on school buses and would leave at the end of the school day. Most girls resided on the fourth floor. The third floor was for girls who were on super good status and were permitted to live more or less without constant supervision. There were partitions separating our sleeping areas, which consisted of two beds and a small wardrobe to be shared, with a full length mirror on the inside.

My living area overlooked the courtyard that was fenced in and had very large, old trees in the center.
My area was level with the tops of the trees. I liked to stare down into that courtyard late at night, especially after it snowed but particularly on full moon winter nights. I loved the way the moon cast shadows from the trees onto the snow-covered ground. I had been trying for a while to put forth a genuine effort to make a go of my surroundings.

Before long though, it seemed like I was getting into trouble all the time again without even trying. The basement was deemed a game/recreation room for residents to hang out and spend evenings and weekends playing board games and watching TV.
As strict as the school was, the actual living environment wasn't that bad. It was hard to believe, but we were allowed to smoke cigarettes. I made several good friends at school and my roommate and I had boyfriends.

I had already attempted to make one getaway. I simply ran out the side door of the school and then ran to the highway in a T-shirt on a 35 degree winter day. Upon emerging by the exit ramp, a cop picked me up. It was strange how quickly he moved in on me. I told him he was wasting his time and I was going to continue to run no matter how many times he picked me up. He told me he was only doing his job and he had to return me to where I belonged.

Living at a school run by penguins was doing more harm than good. It seemed that no one cared how miserable I was. Several months passed by. It got to the point the only reason I went to school was to spend time with my boyfriend. We would sneak off and hide in empty classrooms and stairwells, while skipping classes and capturing each moment we had together during the day.

It eventually began to break my heart at the end of the day when he would get to leave and go home to the free world, while I was left at the parochial prison. We worked on a plan to get my friend and I busted out. The boys usually rode the bus but my boyfriend had access to the use of his father's car. We set a time for eight that evening when we were always in the basement. We made sure we sat at a table in the corner because it was the closest to the ground window.

As the designated time approached, we were wondering if in fact our boyfriends would come through. Suddenly, there was a faint tap at the window. It was them! Our knights in shining armor hadn't failed us! I knew there was no backing out.

We had to get through the door across the room and then we would have to run as fast as we could, pass the matrons on duty, run out of the doors and up the stairs, then into the courtyard. We then had to successfully climb over a 10 foot high chain link fence. We sat there for a few minutes while getting our nerves. We had Lynyrd Skynyrd playing on the cassette player and Gimme Three Steps was on which fired me up even more. I started to worry that our boyfriends would head out on us if we didn't get it into gear, so I asked if she was ready and if she wanted to lead, or if she wanted me to.

We decided I would lead. We tore across that room and it took the matrons a second or two to realize what was happening. We made it past them, pushed the double doors wide-open, jumped out into the snow, and ran as fast as we could to the fence. I interlaced my fingers to give her a cheerleader boost. She made it over and dropped down. I, on the other hand, was teetering on top of the fence halfway over while the matron was pulling hard on my leg.

She held on tight and told me there was no way I was getting away and to get down that instant. I was trying to kick her and kept missing her face by inches. I was mad and cursed at her. She fell backwards and finally let go. I was up and over the top, then dropped hard on the other side. I ran fast into the night to the waiting car across the field.

The three of them were waiting for me in a big, bomber of a car which was running and warm. We were not going to be caught this time so we decided to stash ourselves in the large trunk. Our boyfriends drove us over the New York State line, into Binghamton. We did it! We were free!

We pulled into a liquor store parking lot. One of the guys went in and purchased a fifth of Jack Daniels with a fake ID. We were all going to take a celebration swig, I was last. I took in a big mouthful and immediately began to puke. I had carbon monoxide poisoning from riding in the trunk. I guess I was the closest to the exhaust. I thought I was going to die.

For four straight days, I made the floor of an unknown bathroom my residence. I was very sick. Probably near death. When I came to my senses, I found myself in an apartment that belonged to Laotians, who called themselves boat people. How I ended up there, I have no idea. My friends were long gone and I found myself alone. That was so strange, yet I got up and then thanked my hosts for their incredible hospitality. They barely spoke English.

I made my way to Interstate 81 to hitchhike south as I went past the exit of Lourdesmont and kept going until I reached the exit for Harrisburg. I decided I was going back to visit Earl and Mabel to try and figure out a way for us to get along. When I arrived, at first they were surprised and shocked. They were completely worried because they knew that I was assigned to a placement nearly 100 miles north. I convinced them to let me stay the night.

The next day, I had Earl take me to Carlisle and drop me off at the mall. After window shoplifting a few hours through the mall, I walked slowly downtown to Children and Youth Services to make my presence known. It was apparent I was becoming a thorn in my new caseworker's side. I had already been in nearly every foster home within the central Pennsylvania area. She was now having to find placements for me in different jurisdictions.

I was then placed in a home just outside of Mechanicsburg in the farm country. I liked it because the foster parents pretty much left me alone to do my thing. I mistakenly thought I had established some trust. One Friday night, the foster mom took me to a rollerskating rink and as soon as she pulled away, instead of going skating, I jumped into a car with my friends. We were cruising down the road, when at a stoplight, she pulled up right next to us and gave me some very strong hand gestures to pull over. I was so busted.

I became friends with a girl who lived down the road- she was a wild child like me. She lived with her grandmother in town then came out to the country to spend time with her dad. His house was the one that was next to mine down the road. We would steal his homemade apple and peach wine to spend our afternoons getting drunk while lying out in the sun while he was at work. It was our summer vacation and the world was ours.

I regained some trust with my foster mother and was permitted to attend a Friday night church dance with my friend. We were dropped off and trusted to be on our best behavior. Toward the end of the night, I ended up under a boy in the bushes and lost my virginity. I was so ready, I don't even remember his name. My friend had already had sex a few times and made it sound so exciting and enticing.

I felt that without having been all the way, I had not fully become the woman I knew I was on the inside. My friend's grandma hated me because she thought I was the bad influence. We both knew we got each other into harmless trouble and had fun doing it. I ended up back at Earl and Mabel's house. I was sick of foster care.

CRY TOUGH

I wanted to get a job and go back to school to live as maturely as possible. I could get my own place eventually. I merely needed a spot to crash at night. With all the moving and traveling, I failed seventh grade three times so technically I was still only in eighth grade. I walked into the next town of Lemoyne, where a Hardee's was located.

I applied for a job and was hired. I was then issued a uniform with a name tag and was on my way to independence. I was proud of my first venture of gainful employment as I walked home that night. I managed to convince Earl and Mabel to let me work and not go to school for a while. I wanted to work for my own apartment. They agreed to not rat me out or cause trouble for me.

Earl owned a 1967 Chevy Caprice which I wanted to learn how to drive; I loved that car. It wasn't anything special, it just had nostalgia and that old car smell. He would take me to the cemetery where I would practice my driving skills. Why a cemetery I do not know. I was not allowed to get my permit until I went back to school which was fine. I wouldn't drive.

I worked at Hardee's for a few weeks and became friendly with my boss. We went out once or twice drinking beers, just as friends after work. One night, he handed me a hit of acid and drove me home. That was my first real experience of a bad trip. I sat alone in my bedroom which was still exactly as I had left it years earlier and I stared into a mirror while I watched my face melt.

It was all so grotesque. I stayed in my room and would not come out and then I couldn't stop crying.
Mabel kept knocking on my locked door. I finally had to tell her the truth through the door that I had taken a bad drug and I needed it to get out of my system. I took LSD a few times before, but I had never had an experience like that.

The next day I walked to work for the sole reason of telling my boss that he was a slimeball for giving me a bad hit. I quit after speaking my mind. I wanted to find a part-time job so I decided to keep on walking over the Market Street bridge into Harrisburg. City Island was halfway across. I stopped and went down to walk next to the Susquehanna River to enjoy the sunny afternoon. I then continued to walk into town and came across a very small corner grill called The Spot. It was a local favorite and had been around forever it seemed.

I went in and sat at the counter and ordered a cup of black cup of coffee to accompany the Kool cigarette I was smoking. A jukebox on the wall was playing old 45s. I noticed a guy sitting a few seats away from mine. He was wearing a traditional black leather motorcycle jacket and was drinking black coffee and smoking Kool cigarettes just like me. He resembled the lead singer of Journey. He moved over next to me and we started making small talk. I wasn't familiar with the city streets, so he said he would be happy to show me around. He lived on Third Street, a few blocks away, so we slowly made our way while he showed me the sights. I was in a particular phase at that time, like every other teenage girl wanting to look and imitate Madonna- after all it was the 80s. I was able to afford a few black rubber bracelets in a Chinese owned store that were super cheap.

As we looked through all the stores, there was so much I wanted, needed and desired. Since I quit my job at Hardee's, I would have to search for other means of financial security. Getting a job was my original intention for walking across the bridge. I didn't put in one application that afternoon. We were both tired from walking around, so he invited me to his mom's house to revive for a bit.

As we were walking down the sidewalk, there was a heavyset woman leaning out of a second-story window. She was talking to a man standing down on the street. When she saw her son, she stopped her conversation and razzed him a little to whom his new friend was. She insisted we come up right away while she put on a pot of coffee. I felt like such an adult with this man.

As the lingering day passed by, it began to get dark so I needed to start the long walk home. He insisted on walking me and held my hand the entire way. It was romantic and we fell for each other fast and hard. It was an instant connection. After spending countless days feeling inseparable, we began to spend our nights together too. He was 22.

I would sit out on the front steps of the apartment building, smoking cigarettes to pass the time if he wasn't around to keep me company. This particular part of town had a lot of drugs and promiscuous activity going on in the shadows and pretty much in broad daylight. Prostitutes made their money by walking up and down their blocks. Before long, I got on a first name basis with a few of the dealers and some of the working girls. Some were mothers, others were addicts trying to support an endless habit.

I enjoyed sex, so why not get paid for it? This was the beginning of a whole new world. I wasn't scared, so much as nervous. Sure, I heard stories about freaks doing things like making door handles only open from the outside. Once you were in, there was no way out.

Many days I sat on the imaginary safety line of the front steps, merely watching and observing the girls do their work. I knew as soon as I stepped off and moved to the corner, I was asking for business. What was I doing? Did I care? No, I did not.

The very first time I got into a car was after the trick had circled around the block a time or two. The driver was an old man who I had seen pick up several different ladies. I got in with him because he definitely knew what he was doing. I trusted that he would instruct and guide me on the proper protocol of things I should be doing and help me relax. We cruised around for a while as he informed me of important details like what the undercover cops were driving and who to watch out for in general.

At first, I needed to be coaxed and reminded of how little effort was involved in making twenty or more dollars in fifteen to twenty minutes. Sometimes the time was even less with a blow or hand job. I would have rather had the entire sexual encounter but most of the men that were cruising those streets were only looking for a quick service. Plus, it was easy to cruise and not be noticed. If you were going to do everything- that required a more secluded or discreet location.

I stuck with the basics like jacking them off and I loved the money I was making. Any ugly, old feeling that came to the surface about what I was doing would simply be forced back down into that numb space of my soul. I didn't like working on the streets. Instincts told me that it was far more dangerous getting into random cars rather than other options I could try. I could do the same thing with less risk in other situations.

I met an older woman and began to stay with her. We would put our makeup on and do our hair while she told me stories about going out to the truck stop and rest areas for tricks. She was a lot older than me. She had experience from selling herself for years, so I trusted her guidance. We were both happy to have someone to pal around with while making money and working in pairs is always a good idea. We drove out to the TA truck stop just outside of town.

As we sat in the car, she began to explain how we were going to get started for the night. We sat in the parking lot until we completed touching up our makeup. We then went out to the truck lot and began knocking on doors until some nice driver let us use his CB radio. We offered a minor exchange of services while we looked for someone who might be looking for some company. She told me that I needed a handle.

I needed a name that men could get back to me if they wanted me to take the conversation down to another channel to discuss the details. I decided on the name Green Eyes. With a handle, I was now ready for business. By the end of that first night, I accumulated around $80. The first few nights, we alternated between the truckstop and the local rest areas.

I felt safer at the truckstop. The east and west bound rest areas were always full by nightfall. Despite the plentiful prospects, I always had an extra cautious feeling because the Pennsylvania State Police made regular visits once an hour to mess with drivers or whatever. Sometimes business wasn't good and sometimes everyone seemed to be arrogant and wanted something for nothing.

YOUTH GONE WILD

I did love the big rigs. To me, they were masculine and sexy. Watching a man shift the gears or back it up into a tiny space to park in a more secluded area, became a huge turn on, even if we were called Lot Lizards from time to time. The day came when a driver asked me to travel with him for as long as I wanted. He promised to take care of my needs as far as food and every other expense that may be incurred.

He was very nice, so I agreed. We headed up to New York City and ended up in the Bronx at Hunts Point vegetable market to drop off a load of produce. When he jumped out of the truck and went around to the back to help unload the trailer, he told me to stay in the cab and lock the doors. There were a lot of shady looking characters. Some were men waiting around to be a lumper, which was a man who unloaded the truck for a fee.

I could tell some were homeless and some just looked seriously rough around the edges. After sitting in the cab of the truck for two hours, I became very bored and noticed a deli across the street on the corner. I called the driver back up to the cab and told him I wanted to walk across and get us something to eat for lunch. He tried to convince me to wait but I was starving and told him I needed money to get it. He handed me a $20 and went back to his load.

The minute I jumped down out of the cab and started to make my way to the edge of the fence, the catcalls and wolf whistles began. I don't know why exactly but inside I felt extremely terrified. Maybe I was just reminding myself of how young and vulnerable I actually was. Most of all, I think I was scared of that driver leaving me. What would I do exactly to survive?

As I was waiting for our food, I stood and looked out the front door onto the busy street and decided right then and there – if I was going to survive out here in the real world, I would have to acquire some serious street sense. I would have to avoid large cities, especially this one. I never heard good stories about runaways coming from or going to New York City. A young girl could get lost real quick to the fast pace of drugs or other forms of havoc. Some people could very well have said the life I was living was self-destructive.

I figured as long as I could keep myself from getting killed, I was doing myself justice. The driver and I traveled through a few states, but I guess I grew homesick because I ended up going back to Pennsylvania. I had a taste of the open road and I knew I wanted more. I continued to make trips out to the truckstop to supplement my income. One terrible night, I got into a rig and climbed into the back bunk after a deal was made. The driver pulled out a knife and was going to stab me as he was yelling and saying things like I reminded him of his mother and how he hated his mother.

I feel like my guardian was on overdrive that night. I had the strength to hold that man's hand down that held the knife. I was then able to talk him into calming down enough so at the exact and precise moment, I jumped out of the truck backwards- half dressed. I then raced back to the car sobbing. I couldn't believe that after all of my travels, something so sinister happened in my own hometown. Still, I was infatuated with the road and the easy way in which I was making money.

By this time, I had traveled through 23 states. It didn't matter where the drivers were going, I wanted to see the country. For the most part, my traveling companion's were harmless and gentle souls that had been alone for way too long with just themselves and the highway. At truck stops, the drivers would all work together sometimes in their own way to protect the working girls from obvious threats like security guards, police patrols and assholes.

They even extended the courtesy of walking you to the next truck and made sure you felt safe with the driver. Of course, there was no foolproof method for safety, but I followed the codes that I had learned. Personally, I think my intuition must have been correct and accurate. Or perhaps I was just exceptionally lucky. I never got into a car or truck that made me feel threatened in any way after the one very bad incident.

When I think back to those early days on the road, one of my favorite memories that comes to mind is The Doors, along with abundant sunshine and there was always good music playing like, "Me and Bobby McGee," by Janis Joplin. I always had my bare feet up on the dashboard or hanging out the window. Freedom's just another word for nothing left to lose…

One Saturday morning, I was at the grocery store while tagging along with Mabel. As we walked up and down the aisles, I confessed to her that I had been earning money by selling my body. I assured her that I was completely willing and honestly didn't see anything wrong with it because the men paid me well.

By this time, I knew the value of my worth. She did not want to believe it at first. She didn't particularly approve, yet she didn't not exactly oppose either. I offered her money to help with the bills or anything else she might need, though she declined. I would sit on the back screen porch, overlooking the well manicured backyards of the neighbors and would constantly daydream about being back out on the road and wondered where I would travel to next. I knew I was only taking a breather by coming back to this familiar area. My heart still ached to be wandering aimlessly.

Lynyrd Skynyrd was the main soundtrack to my life. Free Bird was played over and over, along with Tuesday's Gone. I told Earl and Mabel to listen to the words carefully because they did not and could not understand me. I was that Free Bird.

I wore a spiked leather bracelet back to their house one day. I loved it because it went well with black leather, silver studded bustier and my overall style. They were both trying to make me take it off for some reason. For the first time, they both attacked me at the same time. They both swung their fists as hard as they could until they had me down on the floor.

I called them insane freaks and this time, I told them I was leaving and would never come back- they had better pray nothing bad happened to me because they were the reason I willingly chose the streets and the road to get away from them. I met a driver at the truckstop who was going west to Youngstown, Ohio. I asked to ride along and then when we arrived, I would find a ride to continue on with my journey. As we approached Ohio, he was telling me story after story about what a fun party spot the 76 truck stop was, along with some of his favorite memories. In the entire country he told me, it was his favorite stop.

We got there early in the afternoon and because he had time, I could take my time and be choosy with my next destination. I could pick the next driver to get me wherever it was I wanted to get. In the course of the day, we smoked a lot of weed, drank beer and had devilish fun taking turns harassing other drivers on the CB. After all the fun, I wanted to be getting on my way so I began to call out for a ride going anywhere. A sultry voice came back to me on the CB and introduced himself as Bear.

We took it down to another channel because channel 19 was always congested like a busy intersection and hard to get a word in edgewise. He sounded so very sexy and had a southern accent that sweetly rolled off his tongue. He told me his truck was not pretty and as a matter of fact it was downright old, ugly and a cab over.

He drove for his family's company and had intended to only drive this ugly rig a few years until he could buy a nicer truck. This is when conventionals had only been around for a few years and if you had a Kenworth or Peterbilt, you were styling. He assured me that he would take good care of me. He was a relatively new driver and was already sick of traveling alone. There were other drivers that offered me the chance to ride along with them too but Bear seemed the safest.

He walked over to the truck I was in and walked me back to his truck while I was checking him out; not gorgeous, but not gross either. The trailer on his truck was a flatbed and had a huge piece of machinery strapped down to it. Before we left the Youngtown 76 truck stop, he bought a really phenomenal sack of Hawaiian weed, which in my young life thus far, was the best marijuana I had ever smoked. I remember pulling out of there onto Interstate 70 and feeling so high, I wasn't sure I could handle it.

Continuing down the highway we amused ourselves by flashing my titties to unsuspecting truck drivers, as we flew past them in the passing lane, to get them all riled up and talking on the CB. It was summertime and I always managed to drink way too many liquids to be trapped in a rig with nowhere to go and no time to stop, due to a strict schedule. One time, I thought my bladder was going to burst so Bear pulled over onto the shoulder and continued rolling slowly while I opened the door and straddled the open space and I peed while I tried to keep myself balanced.

Within days, we were sleeping together. He didn't want me to have to sell myself anymore so he bought me everything I needed. He bought clothes, makeup and everything else I wanted. It was wonderful to be treated like such a little lady. He took excellent care of me. I stayed with him for several months while traveling all over the country.

The time came when he told me that he had to go home because he was considering a reconciliation with his now ex-wife and he needed to do some work for her around her home. I was bummed. He promised to let me shop at the giant lingerie store that took up two downtown city blocks in his home of Tulsa, Oklahoma. Shopping always made me feel better. I bought several sexy pieces and some fancy shoes. He took me out to a truck stop to find a ride and to send me on my way.

While I had already been having sex with him, he would continually ask me for anal sex. I refused him time and time again. For some reason though, knowing that we were parting ways, I wanted to give him something to remember me by plus I was curious. I think it took some time for me to finally get up the nerve to allow him to do it.

Since the time of losing my virginity under a bush by a boy, it felt like the right time to expand my sexual horizons. I told Bear that I would allow him to have this part of me because this would be our last time together. He was already having sex with a 14 year-old girl and getting this virginal part of me so he was very excited. I don't know exactly what I expected but I did not foresee the way he shoved his way into me. No lubrication, no gentleness.

He went all the way into me without the slightest warning. I felt paralyzed with pain. I could barely get the words out to tell him to stop. I cried a little bit; he held me and then apologized. I then found my ride and we said our goodbyes.

I ended up going to Nashville, Tennessee next. Growing up, I was forced to listen to country music in the car because that is all Mabel would listen to. It did feel pretty spectacular to be in the country music capital of the world. Mabel would likely never get there to visit. She always spoke of her love of the Grand Ole Opry.

The driver I had been riding along with dropped me off at a Motel 6, after checking me in for a week. There was a Waffle House next-door and I ordered grits for the first time. I had never heard or seen or tasted them before. He also left me money to go shopping for more clothes until he returned from spending time with his family. It felt like I was in the true south.

I took a taxi to see all the famous spots around town and bought Mabel a few trinkets, a little keychain and some more memorabilia at a gift shop and then sent them to her. I wanted to rub it in. I think my motives were not pure. I traveled everywhere, going back-and-forth across the country. After a while, I started collecting the cellophanes off of my cigarette packs as I went through each state; it was an easy way for me to keep track of which states I had already been through.

I found myself in Salt Lake City, Utah and we had to pick up a load at a salt mine. Some places were considered hazmat areas and hazmat loads are where drivers would have to drop off or pick up with the regulations much more strict and rigid.

At times, I would have to hide in the bunk area for hours without making a peep. The driver could've gotten into trouble for bringing in a non-authorized person into a secure area. I preferred the places where I could sit openly in the front seat and watch the activity going on. Outside of

Denver, Colorado under a bright full moon, we wound our way down a steep mountain pass. Dream On by Aerosmith was playing loud which helped capture the magic even more.

As I traveled, I remember feeling like I was in a living textbook. I got to see most of the places I read about in grade school. I then found myself stranded in Las Vegas, Nevada. The truck I was in had broken down so I kept walking around, darting into casinos to get out of the 100+ degree heat. Nearly every casino chased me out, while telling me I couldn't be in there without being accompanied by an adult.

I found a man who let me join him. He gave me a bucket of nickels and he let me play right alongside him. We were asked to leave for some reason but he helped me to get a room for me to stay in for the night with no strings attached. The next day I made my way out to the truck stop. Prostitution was legal everywhere but I wasn't old enough to work in a brothel. I also wanted to get out of the sweltering heat of the desert. I couldn't make myself do any tricks anyway.

I got into a blue Kenworth that had Old Crow and Rose Lee hand painted on the side doors.
The driver was an older hillbilly looking man with a long beard. He wasn't bad looking and always wore a brown floppy, leather hippie looking hat and had a mustache and beard. Rose Lee was a young girl, a few years older than me. He had to have been in his 40s.

After we had been traveling together for a few days, we all began sleeping together. Rose and I had designated days and we alternated turns with him. I didn't like it, yet I couldn't wait for the next night to be mine. It was strange, lying there on the bed, while they were having sex. It made me feel all sorts of feelings. I think of jealousy mostly.

They were both from Bakersfield, California. We planned to stay at their house for a few days before returning to the road. We went through Death Valley before passing many wind-powered mills. When we arrived in

Bakersfield, we dropped the trailer and bobtailed to our destination. We walked together into a house where I swear, there were at least 30 people having sex, walking around naked, smoking weed and snorting huge lines of cocaine from piles heaped in the center of tables. They welcomed me like a fresh piece of meat. I was so freaked out I walked straight out of Bakersfield.

Occasionally, I would find myself having to walk many miles on the highway. Those were the times when I would catch rides with cars. I adored the feeling of being one with the road. Sometimes, I was content walking alone for miles and would even refuse rides. There is something about the feeling of just you and the road and your life consisting only of what you can carry.

My favorite time of day to walk was sundown, only because there was a slightly different element of fear to consider. In the night, alone, under the moon and stars was awesome. I was more aware of the snakes that would be trying to warm themselves on the pavement than I was of anything else. It did feel like the bare basics of the road.

It is similar to a biker who rides 1000 miles in order to call himself a true biker. I believed you had to walk miles and miles on the highways before you could call yourself a genuine gypsy.

COMING OF AGE

I steered my course back to Harrisburg to see Butch. Since I was gone he had long since hooked up with another girl, which was perfectly fine with me. I found this out by her coming up to his bedroom while Butch was tattooing me with his name, with a needle and thread. Her arrival made him spill the India Ink. Only a "B" got finished. I later went to a tattoo studio and had the artist write out "Born Wild."

His sister had just moved into a second floor apartment down the street. We had become friends. One day, I was over at her house to help her paint her new place when I heard a motorcycle down on the street, revving the motor and honking the horn, incessantly. It kept going until I shouted down for him to knock it off and stop. He was looking for her and asked if he could come up.

The motorcycle he was riding was black and sleek with chrome and was very loud. When he got up to the apartment, he sat down in the chair in the room I was painting, while carrying on a conversation with her in a different room. He didn't take his eyes off of me the entire time. In between sentences with her, he was asking me questions after introducing himself as Brewster. I liked the way he looked at me and found him mysterious and intriguing.

When he left, he gave me his number and told me to call anytime and he would come to get me. One day, I made that call and as I stood there waiting for him, I was wondering if his invitation could possibly include permanent residency. He arrived on his motorcycle and we strapped my bags down, with one in between us and a pack on my back. We followed the road that ran along the Susquehanna River for many miles. As the sun was setting, we went through the town of Dauphin, then made a turn onto a small country road which was quietly nestled in the valley. It was very peaceful.

We came to a dirt road and turned onto it. On the right was a mobile home and on the left was a metal sign that once said slowdown. Now it said

KKK. Graffiti I hoped. The dirt road continued for a bit across the flatland and fields before it started to ascend up the mountain. He didn't tell me he lived in the woods! I was so impressed.

His house was the very last one at the top of the mountain. On either side of the road, there were several homes scattered at different levels, so everyone had a definite sense of privacy. We pulled onto a stone driveway. His home was very beautiful. It was a two-story with stonework on the base level. There was a garage in the back with the doors open. There was a car under a cover inside.

He pulled back the cover for me to see a gorgeous, pristine 1966 candy apple red Corvette Stingray. From the back of the home, you could look up and beyond to see the summit of the mountain. The back doors were on the same side of the house; the builder put two doors on one side of each other. It looked a little odd and didn't make much sense. Only the one door on the left was ever used. Brewster told me that he had a roommate who lived in the basement but he was very quiet and pretty much kept to himself down there.

As we walked into his home, we were standing in the kitchen. It was open and very spacious with an island in the center. Beyond the kitchen, on the other side of the wall was the living room. There was a bay window overlooking the front yard, which was still only dirt because this was a fairly new build. Beyond the backyard was a backdrop with a magnificent view of the adjacent mountains and valley below.

It all looked wonderful against the evening purple sky from the sun setting in the far off distance. I sat for a few minutes backwards on the love seat looking out and taking it all in. The water to the home was fed from a natural spring; it was all paradise to me. We sat there together and after that we listened to Heart and the Rolling Stones on albums while smoking fat joints. It felt so great, with the cool , free air blowing through the sheer curtains, smelling so evergreen and earthy. We went back out to the bike and got my bags, then brought them in before the nighttime dew fell. The higher elevation made it feel even colder than down below.

He continued to show me through the rest of the house. His roommate was not home so he showed me downstairs in the laundry room as well as the other parts of the home that were not finished. When I asked him why it was unfinished, he said one day he would tell me the story. There were six bedrooms all together, so his room and two others were just beyond the living room. He gave me one of the spare bedrooms.

I liked his bedroom which had natural pine furniture and a red heat lamp above the bed for the main lighting. I noticed the burnt orange crushed velvet bedspread too. I put all my stuff in the room and we made our way back out to the living room. I began to tell him that I really needed a long-term place to stay. I wasn't saying sex was out of the question, but I did express that I did not want to feel pressured into performing, in order to have a place to live.

He made sure that I knew and understood that I was in a safe environment and he was now my friend and he meant me no harm. I could relax and make myself at home, if I wanted a home, I now had it.

NO ONE LIKE YOU

It was September. One more month and I would turn 16. I finally had a home where I could be whomever I wanted and I didn't have to worry about Children and Youth Services. The first few days were heavenly. I was getting settled in while enjoying my new freedom and step up in the world. After a few weeks, I told Brewster that I wanted to sleep in his bed.

After that, we had sex several times a day all over the house. I began spending my nights next to him. We had become a couple. I called Mabel and told her where I was going to live. I was also going to try to get myself enrolled back into high school. She asked me how old he was. I told her he was 36. I also told her that I loved him.

If I had to, I would get him appointed as my legal guardian if she tried to snitch on me to the authorities. I was supposed to be living with them at the moment. She assured me that she would not do anything and hoped I knew what I was doing. I didn't know exactly what I was doing. I wanted to try to have a better life.

I learned fast that Brewster was a drug dealer. That was his main source of income – selling large amounts of cocaine and weed. After a while, I learned to love it when he would bring out the big mirror he had won at a carnival. It had a picture of a naked lady on it and that mirror meant nice big fat lines of cocaine were soon coming. We would do line after line, smoke weed and do shots of Amaretto Di Saronno, Frangelico and have lots of sex.

I had often mentioned to him that I had aspiring dreams of becoming a model. Earlier in life I was in a runway fashion show for JCPenney and got to keep what I modeled. I liked to be photographed. He went out and bought a 35mm camera. It turned out the bedroom was a perfect photography studio. The lighting made me look angelic. I had acquired quite a collection of lingerie and recently began collecting sexy boots and shoes. I loved to make my makeup look professional and dramatic.

We began the very first photo shoot with a Polaroid. I liked the instant gratification and seeing what I was doing right or wrong in each shot. Before long, we had an extensive collection of nude and semi-nude shots. I loved the way I looked. I felt completely confident with my body and so beautiful and sexy.

The way Brewster interacted with me helped me relax and helped me let out my inner sex vixen. I was playfully willing to bare all. We would go to an NHSA show and before long, I was smiling in my bikini and lingerie by the owner's car. We were selling packages of one poster and 10 single shots – two each of five different poses. I was making a lot of money.

 At one show, the people who displayed the ZZ Top car asked me to pose with it. That was a huge moment for me. Brewster and I created a portfolio that consisted of over 200 photos. Each with unique poses. We were going to go through the process of having me emancipated so I could have a chance to pose in the big sex magazines like Cheri, Oui and maybe even Hustler. If I had to wait two years until I turned 18, that would be fine.

After the summer ended I got myself back into high school. I took a test which placed me into the 10th grade. I failed the seventh grade three times, then skipped eighth and ninth grade.
Central Dauphin High School was down in Harrisburg. I was still a ward of Children and Youth Services but because I was attempting to do everything I could right, they stayed off my back. There was only one catch- I wasn't placed into the mainstream classes of high school.

I was in a special education class with the Capital Area Intermediate Unit that held most of the curriculum in one classroom. A few subjects were taught outside of that one room. Brewster bought an old car for me to drive down the mountain each morning to meet the school bus on the lower road. After school, he would sometimes pick me up on his bike.

It used to make me feel pretty different because all of the other kids would be standing there waiting for buses or their parents outside of school and he would come roaring in on the motorcycle and off we would go. It felt great when the kids would ask if he was my father and I would tell them no, he was my boyfriend. After school, if I wasn't riding my dirt bike, I was shooting beer cans with Brewster's .38 pistol. I think I liked to shoot a little too much at that time. I know there weren't too many teenagers that could claim they spent their afternoons like I did or their nights.

My teacher, Ms. Yearnsley was and still is one of the classiest ladies I have ever met. She was a petite black woman with a very good fashion sense and charm and I could also see she had loads of female charisma. She walked like a professional model with so much grace. I watched her walk down the hallway one day, back to our classroom and saw how confidently she carried herself in her femininity. She was the woman who taught me how to carry myself like a lady- to talk and walk and to dress like a classy lady.

Ms. Yearnsley and I became friends. She knew that I was mature beyond my years and treated me as such. She made me feel like a young lady. She made me have aspirations to graduate and make something of myself. She took me home with her a time or two or let me ride along with her while she picked up her children from daycare.

Through her patience and determination for me to succeed, she helped me go from dropout status to the Honor Roll within the first year I was in her class. I was proud but I still couldn't shake the bad girl image of myself all together. During our lunch break, my friend Marci and I would go into the bathroom to smoke our cigarettes. We got caught a few times already so now we stood up on the toilet so we could see over the stalls to see if it was a teacher or a narc coming in. My outfit of choice now was black spandex pants with black boots, a tank top with a baggy flannel shirt over it.

Marcy had gotten a car so we didn't have to hang around the school campus if we didn't want to and we usually didn't. We cruised around with Metallica blaring on the speakers of her little Volkswagen Rabbit. Marcy would bring me home occasionally and would stay to visit and party before heading back to Harrisburg. Brewster shot a few dozen erotic photos of us together. We thought we looked so hot with our matching root perms and bleach blonde hair which we made stand straight up when we teased it with hairspray.

Definitely 80s hair band material. Poison was a local band. Their album, Look What The Cat Dragged In was beginning to pick up steam and Marci and I listened to it religiously. We had the band sign our bellies at the Capitol City Mall while they were doing a promotion for the album. When the event was over, Marci and I ripped our high-heeled boots off and ran like hell, along with two hundred other girls, through the mall to the front parking lot where their tour bus was. Marci and I were so first that we got to make out with them. I had Bobby Dall who asked me when he could rape me. As much as I wanted to, I said no. Iron Will. Velvet Glove.

Earl began occasionally coming to pick me up at school. I think he was attempting to spend some quality time together. He would let me drive to their house to have dinner or whatever. Earl began occasionally coming to pick me up at school. I think he was attempting to spend some quality time together. He would let me drive to their house to have dinner or whatever.

I was able to get my actual drivers license soon after. Brewster always welcomed Earl and Mabel into his home. I still had mixed feelings, so I was just trying to make some sort of effort towards peace. Our house was beginning to turn into a major party destination. People were coming to buy cocaine or weed all throughout the day. Brewster would always ask them to stay and party a little bit before they headed out. One night, someone brought a Turkish water pipe that had five hoses and mouthpieces attached- we all got super high by adding weed, then hash with a sprinkle of cocaine on top.

Our roommate began to join in on our sexual festivities and then before I knew it, I was having sex with three men and one woman. I am pretty sure that it is classified as an orgy, but by now I think I really liked it. At some point, Brewdter began to set me up for dates with some of his high rolling, high-profile clientele, like an escort service. I could not have been more content with myself: I was 16 years old and making $140 an hour. I dated a lawyer who later hooked me up with two other attorneys.

There was even a doctor. I did this for a while, but deep down, I still hated pulling tricks, which is all the fancy dates really were. Each and every man claimed they would take good care of me if they could be my regulars.

I was still enrolled in high school and I was now in the 11th grade. My friends and I were all standing in a circle one day smoking a joint just outside the entrance doors. The principal stepped out and caught me with the joint in my hand. I knew he was going to have my locker searched, which held an ounce of weed I was going to attempt to sell. What I'm about to tell you may not sit well, but please see the good.

Ms. Yearnsley took the sack of weed and hid it for me in the teacher's bathroom trash can because it would have been an automatic expulsion for me. She put everything on the line for me, along with the teaching position she had worked so hard for. She later told me the reason. She knew how hard I had worked to pull up my grades in an attempt to have graduation in mind. She protected me so I would stay in school and get a diploma. She knew I had only made a mistake that day.

I did get suspended for the joint for three days. The days off of school were a welcome break to clean my house and get things organized. I was beginning to not like my life but I was hanging on by a very thin thread. Brewster and I came home one night from a grocery trip and saw the door was wide open. When we walked in, all the drugs were gone, along with $12,000 cash.

The house was ransacked. My jewelry was missing as well as other valuables. We had been robbed. Exactly one week later, we were in the living room having conversations with our roommate, when all of a sudden all three of the doors were kicked in at the same time. I ran to the bay window to look down into the front yard.

There were at least 15 military looking men dressed in black with giant guns pointing towards the house. They came through the doors, rushing in and screaming commands for us to get on the floor. Before I knew it, I had a female DEA agent on top of me, sitting on my back before she gathered my hands to cuff me. The three of us simply lay there and looked at each other from floor level. The parties with sex, drugs and rock 'n' roll were gone forever. Of course, as they were searching through all of our belongings, they found the multitude of half nude photos of me.

They also decided to tack on a child pornography charge along with the drug charges. When it was time for Brewster to appear in court, I had to testify in order for the child porn charges to be dropped. He had a combination of other charges including possession of illegal firearms. I insisted on having the photos taken. They agreed to drop the child pornography charges.

I went to stay with Earl in Mabel for a few days. I was pretty much spooked and I would now have to live at that house alone, which didn't thrill me. I had the bus pick me up from their house- I took the short bus to school, no joke. My driver was a hippie living in the wrong era, who would give me one hit of acid each morning. In school, while I was tripping, I would have to wear sunglasses because I was so wasted and everything was so bright besides the colors and fun trails. Ms. Yearnsley always knew when I was on something.

In those days, she would keep me contained with her in her classroom, instead of my going to my mainstream classes throughout the day as usual. Mabel would take me over to Harrisburg to visit Brewster in the Dauphin County Jail. He began to get very controlling and his personality was becoming different. Maybe it was me that was becoming different. I sold his Corvette for him, which brought in $16,000 to pay for his massive attorney fees.

The court offered him a plea bargain if he agreed to be an undercover informant; he would then receive a lesser sentence. He would have to wear a wire and participate in sting operations. During the time he would be assisting the police, they thought it would be best to keep him incarcerated to protect him better after each bust. It was also so no one would know of his involvement in some instances. I knew what happened to snitches. I think ending up in ditches was the nice part of the story. I didn't want to think about what I was getting caught up in.

A few weeks after, I sat there all alone in the house in complete silence. I did not want to wait around for anyone to come after me for his stupidity so I packed up my things and I left. I went to school the next day and told my teacher that I had to go. I just couldn't hold out any longer. I needed to be on the road somewhere.

The road called for me, like a song. Ms. Yearnsley begged me to stay and graduate because I had made it so far and was so close to my final year of education.

There were no excuses to be made, I quit officially the next day. Before I quit, I had a meeting with the Board of Education in the school to go over all of my awesome progress. Ms. Yearnsley and I did not want to mention my intention to leave. A few months earlier while I was sitting in in-school suspension, I wrote a poem and felt compelled to share it
with the board members and most of all my beloved teacher. It read as follows:

You Say You Want To Help Me
And Lead Me To The Right Way
If You Truly Are Sincere
Don't Mold Me
Like I Am Clay
Don't Tell Me Any Secrets
Nor Tell Me Any Lies
This Dream I Have
Will Not End
Until I Am Satisfied
I Am Like The Break Of Dawn

Waiting To Rise And Be Seen
It Seems As If
My Nights Never End
Just To Hold Me Back From My Dreams
I Wear A Mask, A Special Mask
So No One Can See Who's Behind
Eventually Like Everything Else
It Gradually Dissolves With Time
Then I Am Left Standing There
With No One By My Side
There Is Nowhere To Turn
Nowhere To Run
Then There Is Nowhere To Hide

The education board was very impressed with my academic success story and looked forward to my graduation. They knew of all the obstacles I had to deal with in order to return to my education. It felt great to be acknowledged for my hard work, yet my mind was made up. This would be my very last day in school – no one was going to change my mind.

I called Mabel and asked her to do whatever she had to do to assist me to get my emancipation. I had turned 17 and I was done with foster homes. I wanted to make it official now. I wanted to be set free and treated like the adult I was. A few days had passed since I made the call to Mabel and I wasn't fully sure I could trust her. When she called back, she gave me the news: I was emancipated from the system.

My current boyfriend was beginning to be a drag, so I decided to make my way out to the nearest highway exit with a friend so we could hitchhike. I didn't realize how far out into the country our ride would have to go to get to an exit. We left late in the afternoon and arrived around 4 PM. The weather was sunny and warm at first but then the temperature dropped dramatically. It was early evening and by nightfall, a winter storm blew in.

The temperature dropped drastically and for some bizarre reason we could not get a ride. It was nearly dark, so we started to head back down the country road. We were walking and stumbling for over an hour when it began to snow hard. I was not wearing a coat, hat or gloves.

We had no idea that snow was on the radar. After having walked for three hours against the wind and snow, we began to feel like hypothermia was setting in and maybe frostbite. I was beginning to get scared. We came to an intersection that had an old, wooden bus shelter on the side of the road. We tried to crouch down but the snow was still blowing in on us. Even though the wind was partially blocked, the snow hitting my skin felt like stinging ice needles.

We then noticed a barn across the street so we ran inside. It was late and I was seriously freezing by this point. I was trying to use the very minimal heat of a lighter to at least try to warm our hands, which would not stay lit from the wind. We were in a bad situation and getting desperate. There was a farmhouse across from the barn with light still on inside.

I knew we had to get to the house and ask for help. Feeling weak, I ran to the front door and knocked. A woman opened the door and then her husband came up behind her.

I tried to explain through my shivers that we became stranded in the storm. They allowed us to come inside, showing us to the kitchen where we sat around the kitchen table. They were each in their bed clothes as it was pretty late. They seemed to be sympathetic to our plight. The woman even prepared hot chocolate.

I asked if they could give us a ride into town, after trying to call my boyfriend several times. He was not at home. It felt so good to finally feel some warmth in my body again. Then they did the unimaginable! They sent us back out into the storm. When you get temporarily warmed up, it only makes the snow pelting your skin feel even worse. They wouldn't even provide me with a coat.

After walking for nearly another hour back towards town, not one single car passed by.

I think hypothermia was definitely setting in because I saw headlights coming slowly up behind us but I really wasn't sure if it was real or not, like I was hallucinating or something. As the light got closer to us I laid down in the middle of the road. I felt like I was going to die anyway so this was our last resort.

I remember just lying there with little strength to move in the bright glow of the headlights as they got closer. Still doubting my mental faculties, I wondered if it was only the white light. My guardian was definitely there with me. I regained complete consciousness in my boyfriend's apartment with a pile of blankets on top of me. Amazingly, it was a doctor who picked us up.

I don't even know how I ended up in his car, never mind back at the apartment. I hung in there for some time after that but I again quickly grew bored and headed out.

WILD SIDE

I went to a New Year's Eve party and met a Native American guy, whose name was Sage. We ended up getting down in the bathroom by the end of the night. We were both in lust and pretty much after that night, we were just good friends with benefits.

We went to visit Earl and Mabel for me to say goodbye. We decided we were going to pull all of our measly funds together and head our way down to Florida for Daytona Bike Week.

It was a hell of a lot warmer and we wouldn't have to worry about being out on the streets in the cold and snow. Earl gave us a ride out to the truck stop and dropped us off. I was eager to get on the road and to be headed south. I knew I wasn't going to see Earl for a long time, so it was one of those goodbyes. I still despised him deep down but I was on my way to a new life yet once again.

Sage and I left with $20 after I got ripped off for $10 from some guy that sold me bunk Lebanese blond hash. We scored a dream ride with a driver going all the way to Ormond Beach, just outside of Daytona.

It was really hard to find a ride at first. When a female gets on the CB asking for a ride, in most instances she would receive numerous responses. A female asking for a ride with a male companion is an entirely harder process to get to where you are going.

However, we were on the road by two in the morning. We both sat in the passenger seat until we were out of Virginia. I couldn't believe how quickly the miles were passing by. The driver definitely had his hammer down. I crawled to the back and got into the bunk. I was exhausted, so the driver told me to get some sleep.

The rocking rhythm of the 18-wheeler making its way down the highway, became my favorite sweet lullaby over the years. When I awoke a few hours and many miles later, it was nearly 11 o'clock the next morning. We pulled into a truck stop somewhere in South Carolina. I made my way to the restroom to freshen up and change my clothes that I had now been wearing for three days straight. I didn't like the way I smelled so I stood there and washed as discreetly as I could, while ladies came and went.

I dried my wet body parts with the hand dryer on the wall. I came out feeling so refreshed and felt new again, ready to take on the world. Sage and I entertained ourselves in the drivers lounge playing video games and watching television, while we waited for the driver. He bought us a huge dinner then filled his coffee thermos and we were on our way.

From Pennsylvania, we ran Interstate 95 the entire way down the coast. It was not a terribly long trip at all. The driver pulled over next to a gas station to let us out on Highway US1, a straight shot to all the fun and festivities but most importantly, Daytona. I thanked the driver for his genuine kindness and especially for carrying us the entire length of our journey, which made life so much easier. He handed me a $20, then I got out of the truck and hurried to a very plush patch of green grass and sank down, rolled around and kissed the ground and felt so blessed by the green earth.

We made it to Florida! It felt like a different world because it was. I went into the single, smelly outside entrance restroom while Sage stood outside and guarded the door so I could freshen up. I set my backpack on the sink, which in the outside pocket held a brand new intricate hand blown glass bowl I had bought before the trip to smoke some good Florida weed out of. Then just like déjà vu – it flipped off the edge of the sink onto the pocket the bowl was wrapped up in. My efforts of protection did not work. Instead of handling a solid piece of glass, I picked up a smashed pile of glass. I threw it in the trash, sad that I never even got to use it.

I should have known this was an ominous welcome that Florida had to offer. We began our long walk into town. The closer we came to Daytona on the Mainland side the more visible the street people and drug dealers became. The serious prostitutes were obviously on their turf because they were everywhere and did not appear to be concerned about the police. I could also tell this was the poorer area of town. I wanted to keep walking before any trouble came our way.

We had around $14 left, so for the moment it seemed like we were ok. We walked from the mainland to the beachside then we made our way to A1A, also known as the strip. The main reason for my wanting to arrive precisely at this time was Daytona Beach Bike Week. I had done my research by asking various bikers about it before I left Pennsylvania, so I was moderately informed. We arrived at the very tail end of Race Week after the Daytona 500 so we could get situated somewhere before the big motorcycle event.

The bikers were just beginning to filter in. It was about half Nascar fans and half bikers at this time.
The only thing you can do when you're broke and homeless in Daytona Beach is wander around constantly. On the beach side, if you didn't have enough money in your pocket, they could arrest you for vagrancy. Sage seemed to have no problem finding places for us to crash but he would always end up leaving me somewhere just so he could go off with the hard-core partiers. We would meet up later, usually at McDonald's. Within a few days Mc Donald's became more or less of a homebase.

I lost nearly all of my clothes somewhere along the way, so I had only one pair of jeans and two or three shirts, which I wore in layers when I got cold at night.
It is hard to put into words what you feel as you walk around aimlessly, always trying hard to fit in. The families up on the boardwalk who are buying their children ice cream cones or paying for rides and games are full of joy and laughter. A lot of feelings come over you when nightfall comes. You can sit on the sand and hear all of the activity going on around you. The black night can intensify the sadness you feel from not being able to participate.

That I believed, was the beginning of the end for life on the street for me as I had known it. It didn't matter how broke I was, I could eat by paying with change I found on the street or asked for. At the end of the day, I would hike my soap and shampoo into the Ladies Room, where mothers were helping their kids go potty. There I was, washing my long hair in the sink and then blow drying it under the hand dryer.

We lived on the streets hard-core for about 2 1/2 months, making it all the way through Bike Week into Spring Break. By the time all the rich, preppy college kids arrived, I definitely had enough of the streets. I also told Sage that I couldn't deal with his excessive partying, and it would be best if we parted ways. I met two guys who were headed towards Tampa. I asked if I could ride along. The streets of Daytona kicked my ass. I was sick of struggling to survive. It is a town that will chew you up and spit you out if you are not careful.

Unlike on the mainland side, if you were a single woman, walking along A1A, beach side, you were going to be harassed by the cops. I think I did a trick or two to get by, but for the most part I was determined not to have to do that anymore. Broke or not. That is the reason why Tampa began to sound so good to me. All the jobs in Daytona were pretty much spoken for at the beginning of the season.

I just didn't have it in me to live on the streets and get it together enough to get a real job. When we first arrived in Tampa, we drove through a small trailer park just south of Highway 41. Tampa Bay and the harbor were just down the road. The person we were looking for in the trailer park wasn't at home so we went up to the corner bar and grabbed two six packs of beer and went down to the docks.

The sun was going down, and as we sat on the dock over the water, I couldn't help but think of Otis Redding. As I sat there, with his song rolling through my mind; yes, I guess this is where I belonged, sitting on the dock of the bay.

FALLEN ANGEL

One night, I met a man who told me he worked on one of the shrimp boats I saw in the harbor. He invited me to come onto the boat and party. It was interesting but being on a shrimp boat the stench was horrible. He asked if I had ever done cocaine. I answered yes. He then asked if I ever shot up. I answered that I never had.

He offered to give me a boot if I wanted to try. I asked if I could just snort some and he said I could, if I really wanted to, but it was so much more intense if you shot it up. I agreed to give it a try. He put a band around my upper arm then gave me what he said would be just enough for a good high. The one important detail he forgot to mention was when you shoot up, it makes you instantly puke. How sickening it was to smell the shrimp while hurling over the edge of the boat. I never shot up again.

One afternoon, I was reading through the newspaper, looking for a job. I couldn't help but notice how many ads there were for exotic dancers. They all claimed that a girl could easily make at least $1500 a week. I continued looking for a regular job and kept making calls. I couldn't get that image of having $1500 a week of pay out of my mind. I wanted to make that kind of money. I needed that kind of money.

All the ads included the words, No Experience Necessary. I began calling some of the clubs I realized that one of them was located right up the street from me. I could take the bus if I needed to. There were two shifts, the first shift was one in the afternoon to eight in the evening; the second shift was from seven at night to three in the morning. I wanted to work the first shift. When I called, I spoke with the owner, whose name was Larry.

He offered to come pick me up and take me to the club to show me around. When he arrived, I invited him in for a drink. I told him I had absolutely no experience whatsoever with dancing. I never even went to a high school dance. He told me a lot of the girls had no experience when they first started. Now they were all making well over $1000 a week. Sounded great to me. He then asked if I was comfortable being nude.

This was after all, an all nude club. I told him that I thought I could be comfortable so he told me to strip right there, in front of him. It struck me a bit then he said he had to make sure I had a nice body and no horrible scars or anything like that. It made sense to me so I stripped for him.He was sitting in my recliner and waved for me to come closer to him.

As soon as I was within arms reach, he began playing with one of my nipples to make it hard. I looked at him funny. He told me not to worry, he was friendly like this with all of his girls and then he told me to relax and not be so uptight. We got into his Lincoln and headed north to the club. The building was painted black and there was an outside sign, with bright lights around the border, which read, Fantasy Men's Club.

Little did I know, this was one of the worst clubs in Tampa. It was a starting point. There were signs that advertised "Live Nude Shows and Beautiful Ladies. It made me feel glamorous even though the overall building looked run down. When we walked in, it was very dark and it took a few moments to get my eyes to adjust. When I could finally see again I saw to my left, a room lit with dim red light with bench seats along the walls. Several men had their backs against the wall, while naked ladies gyrated all over them.

As we stood there at the cash register, I couldn't help not to stare at everyone and everything going on. I had never seen such a sight. Larry introduced me to the manager before we walked into the main bar area- off to the left was the juice bar as it was a BYOB type of bar. In front of us, was a large stage with the jukebox behind it against the wall which played 45 rpm records. Three songs for $1.00. All around the stage were chairs with men mingling, amidst half naked women.

On the right, against the back wall, was a smaller stage and in between stages were pool tables. The dressing room and ladies restroom were in the back. Larry escorted me into the dressing room. Two walls had mirrors with hair dryers and curling irons plugged into nearly every outlet. The smell of different perfumes lingered in the air. On the floor were bags with costumes spilling out along with accessories.

There was a couch in the center of the room that looked like I wouldn't want to sit on it without something between my skin in the cushions. He introduced me to the girls that were tending to themselves, preparing to go on stage. Larry told me that I had to sign some paperwork, including a contract. As we walked back through the club to his office in the far corner, some of the men stopped their conversations and asked when I was going on stage. They stated they had some bills with my name on them.

They said they didn't know my name-hell- I didn't even know what my stage name was going to be. Just like choosing a CB handle, you want a name that describes you. The women accompanying those particular men did appreciate their clients' attention to me. I even received a few mean looks. Larry opened the door to his office and we went in. It was ice cold in there, with his air-conditioner blasting, so it felt nipply . It was nearly 100° outside but it didn't matter.

There was a large, brown leather couch in front of his desk. He told me to sit down as he went around the desk and sat in his chair, in front of me. We sat there for a few minutes when he finally said, " You really are very pretty. "You will make a lot of money if you learn how to hustle. At this club, these women know how to hustle." I didn't know what that meant. He then walked back around his desk and reached into his drawer to pull out some paperwork. The first page was the contract.

The main stipulation was by signing this contract I was forbidden to work in any other club. If I did, I would be forfeiting my contract and would be banned from working at Fantasy's ever again. I could deal with that. There were other rules and regulations that had to be followed or I would be subjected to fines. The fines could range from $15 to $100, depending on the infraction. I read the contract over and then signed but then there was a legal adult form that required my identification to be photocopied.

I lied and told him that my purse had recently been stolen, but once I could get my birth certificate and Social Security card, I would be able to provide proper identification. It seemed to pose no problem at the time, except for the little fact that I had only just turned 17. I lied again and said that I had just turned 18. I told Larry I needed this job desperately and I would do anything to keep it. That was a bad choice of words, considering the type of guy Larry was.

We finished up the paperwork and afterwards he asked me what my stage name would be. After a few moments of serious contemplation, I told him Lacey. He then came back around his desk and sat down on the couch beside me. He asked if I would be willing to give him a blow job. He was fat but clean and smelled good. I started to give him a blowjob and then jacked him off.

We both sat there for a little while then he told me that he had some outfits that I could look at which I could eventually purchase, if I wanted to. For now, I could borrow them. He even had shoes which most likely had been left behind by previous dancers who had been fired, or their property had become collateral. I asked him not to tell anyone what we had done in his office. I then asked if that act was expected of me with the customers. He said no, but it was expected of him.

He also said that I would be his special girl and he would come pick me up every day and be lenient on me in other ways for taking care of him. As we walked out of the office, all eyes were on me. It felt as though everyone knew what I had done. He told me to go back to the dressing room, get makeup on and get glamorous. I sat in that dressing room for two hours. I was so nervous!

By the time I was finally ready, it was almost 6pm. I was told the bar always picked up around this time of night because guys would stop in after work. It was about halfway packed when I stepped out onto the floor and the atmosphere was fun and everyone was having a good time. Even though there was the old jukebox which the dancers had to feed dollars into, there was a DJ announcing which girl was coming up onto the stage next. I finally got myself relaxed enough by drinking a few shots in my juice. I told the customers that this was my first time up on stage.

I walked over to the jukebox, to pick my favorite music and then told The DJ I was ready. This is it. I'm doing this. Here I go! The first song I picked was, Touch Me by Samantha Fox. As the girl on stage was collecting her dollars, the DJ started getting the crowd ready for me. I was trembling. All I could do and hope for is that I did not trip or anything dumb like that.

The first song of your set you keep all of your clothes on, the second song you keep only your bottoms on, fully topless. By the third song you are to be completely nude. When the third song came on, I was surprised at how much it didn't bother me to be nude in front of a bar full of strange men. I made $120 in two hours that night after tip out. Tip out included 10% of what you made going to the DJ, 10% went to the waitress that served you the most throughout the night and 5% went to the bouncer and doorman.

I was hooked! I was finished with my audition around eight that evening. Eastlake Mall was right across the street. I ran over and couldn't wait to spend my money. I knew I had to put some dance outfits together that were my own creations. I tried to find stores that carried sexy lingerie and thongs.

Right from the beginning I knew I wanted to stand out from the rest of the girls. In this business, you had to get creative in order to draw the man's attention away from the other girls. Most of the girls did not catch onto this so in my opinion, they all looked the same or at least looked like they all shopped at the same stores. I was always talented when it came to taking a pair of scissors to clothing! I liked the wild, ripped look. Before long, I had a dance bag full of outfits and I was working every single day. Some days I worked double shifts.

I had my own trailer now in the mobile home park. It was cheap. I only had to pay $60 a week. My friends had moved on, so I worked every day and shopped every night. I never saved my money. I always found justification to spend it.

When I did come across drugs, I made myself quit after a few hours or days. I never spent my money on drugs in order to cope with life, like most dancers. After that first night of having to get slightly intoxicated to get my nerve up to go on stage, there was no need to drink. I put myself in many different dangerous situations so I wanted to have my wits about me. The majority of my money went towards makeup, styling products, clothes and pretty much everything having to do with beauty and living large with glitz and glamor.

I loved to make sequin embellished outfits, even if only with a glue gun. I wasn't overly keen on wearing gowns or dresses at the high-class clubs. I sought out the clubs where I could be comfortable and flattered by my unique wild child style. I wasn't quite ready to change stages yet though. I learned how much I loved to perform on stage.

I didn't just get up there and shake my ass- I learned to dance beautifully. It was my world up there and sometimes I wouldn't even care if they tipped me or not. Guys would get insulted and frustrated, waving their bills, while calling me over to them. After a while the euphoria of dancing my troubles away, while being drenched in sweat at the end of my sets made me feel like I had the world by the balls. Literally. It was a way for me to feel the power over men.

Private dances were an entirely different arena. 1 for $20. 2 for $30. 4 for $50 and on and on. Mind you, it was 1987. I learned to become a proficient actress. As your thighs are in between the customers legs while rubbing his hard-on through his pants using only your knees as you hovered over him, you have the power to make all his wild fantasies come true with nothing but the seduction of your voice.

Two months passed by, and Larry was getting impatient for me to produce my identification. I told him I would take a leave of absence, while I worked on it and I would gladly take a small vacation. I was sick of servicing him anyway. In the end, he started to become a jerk when I would refuse, so the fines started to accumulate. I grew to hate him.

All the while I was gaining experience and pole skills so when I hit legal age, I knew I could work in any club I chose. In the meantime, I had to lay low for a while because of the fact I never saved any of my money and subsequently lost the trailer.

WHEREVER I MAY ROAM

I found myself back at square one. Broke and ready to hit the highway. Within walking distance of the club and mall was a fairly new truckstop called Cigar City on Hillsborough Avenue. My intention was to find a driver to let me use his CB in order to get a ride anywhere but there. I went into the restaurant with my backpack and ordered a plate of fries and a Coke.

Everyone was looking at me as though I was out of place. I finished eating, then went into the game room to look for a driver to ask if I could use his CB radio. I found one and as we walked out to his truck, everyone looked at me like I was a working girl. Maybe I was. A loud voice came over the CB, stating he was looking for trucks he could do his artwork on. He had an echo box, so it boomed above the others. The man said he did glass etching , airbrush work, pinstriping and occasional wheel polishing.

I got on the CB and started talking to him when he revealed he didn't have any potential clients at the moment. He told me where his van was parked and said I could come over and hang out with him if I wanted to. It was almost dark so I agreed. We sat there in the truck stop parking lot, talking for a few hours when I told him I didn't have any place to stay.

He rolled us a joint and then said he would rent a room for me there at the truckstop motel. He could get a special rate since he was the person who had painted all their signs and brought trucks in to have artwork done. He let me know he wasn't looking for sex but he did request that if I was trying to find tricks that I instead just stay in the room and not work, wander or let anyone in. He told the management that I was his niece or something. I assured him he had nothing to worry about.

We walked over to the store and bought some snacks for me to have for the night. He left me his home phone number and told me to call if I needed to. The next morning Coyote gave me his real name and I was properly introduced to him as Rich. He showed up with coffee and McDonald's in hand. He said if I wanted to, I could hang out with him for the day. That was the day I almost died of heat stroke! The high temperature and Florida humidity did not agree with me at all.

The fact that I was sitting in a metal van that added 20° to the already 100° temperature with 90% humidity proved a bad combination for me. Rich didn't seem to mind it at all as his skin was dark bronze and had a leather appearance. He wasn't muscular but didn't have any fat on him and was rather tall and lanky. He knew I was only 17 so he told me his age, which was 35. He told me he was an Army medic in the Vietnam War and other details about himself. I watched him work all day and was impressed with his skills.

He fed me and made sure I had plenty of fluids to keep me from dying of dehydration. At the end of the day he offered to let me come and stay at his house for a while until I could get on my feet again. He went on to tell me about his town of Gibsonton, which was about 10 miles south of where we were in Tampa. His mobile home had two bedrooms and rent was only $75 a week. The first night when we arrived at his trailer, I felt pretty comfortable. Walking inside, I found it to be cool and clean.

I kicked off my shoes and after we got stoned, he invited me to sit and keep him company while he threw some sandwiches together for us. He asked if I wanted a glass of milk, then poured one for me. Over the next few days, when he would get ready to leave for work, he expected me to go with him. He still wasn't completely comfortable leaving me alone in his home. I couldn't blame him, and it didn't offend me. After all, he had nice things that could easily go to a pawn shop.

A Friday night came when Rich told me we were invited to a party somewhere on Fowler Avenue in North Tampa. In the time we had spent together, thus far, I thought he was pretty much only a stoner. At the party, there was a guy who was selling grams of cocaine. Rich bought one then another and then another! Before we knew it, he had blown over $700 on the stuff!

We were both wasted, but we were having a blast. The pool was in the backyard and everyone was cooking out and drinking off of a keg and having a good time. Eventually, with that kind of money spent, it was time to leave, with about a gram and a half of cocaine left. We ended up on the edge of the bay, in the back of the van on the bed watching the rain pouring down outside. We sat on that bed and continued to snort line after line until the powder was gone. After that, we got into some really deep conversations about anything and everything. Before I knew it, I was crying.

Then we kissed and made love.I thought it was definitely love. I wanted so desperately to not be on the streets anymore and I thought this was my chance to have a normal life in a real home. I officially became the woman of the house in the beginning of September. When he went to work, I would stay home. On October 9th, I turned 18.

Trouble began brewing right from the beginning. He wanted to argue about subjects that warranted no dispute. He began to get more possessive and controlling by putting me down and reminding me where I came from. I was in another abusive relationship but I didn't know it at that time. I did my best to be a good girlfriend but he was never happy. After a lengthy and heated argument because he refused to get a real job, I left him and returned to Pennsylvania.

Two weeks later Rich called and begged me to come back, then he even asked me to marry him. I did return to Florida and on November 12, 1987 our first child was conceived. I drove myself to the doctors office, only to wait patiently to be seen for two cracked ribs from a fall from Tequila. The doctor asked if I was late for my menstrual cycle. I confirmed yes, it was a few days late. He said he wanted to perform a blood test to rule out pregnancy, which is how I learned I was pregnant.

The morning sickness came soon after and would not cease. I became so dehydrated from vomiting, I had to be hospitalized for a few days to replenish all the fluids I had lost. I felt the need to bring the baby into a healthy living environment so it only made sense to me that Rich and I should be married as he suggested before, to get me to come back. Considering the fact that only a few months earlier he had tried to convince me to abort, I suppose marriage was a foolish notion from the start. The abortion issue was one of the major disagreements we had.

Justin was born on August 18th, 1988 after I got through the ordeal of an 18-hour labor that turned into an emergency Cesarean birth. After administering an epidural and several hours of pushing, the doctor discovered that I had Cephalopelvic disproportion; a childbirth complication. It happened because my baby couldn't pass through the opening in my pelvis. It felt so strange lying there on the operating table, going from a full participant in my child's birth to now having everything completely out of my control.

As the doctor tugged at my belly, I had a barrier/shield in front of my face to not see what the doctor was doing. Rich was able to see and watch everything. I felt deprived and cheated and it didn't really feel fair. I was, however, able to truly appreciate what I had done, bringing this tiny soul into the world.

From there our arguments only became worse. Abortion was simply not a part of my credo. I felt very blessed to be chosen to bring a soul into the world. Rich was not happy with the idea that we were to be parents from the beginning.

I heard that a local Tampa Bay radio station was sponsoring a promotional mass wedding for Valentine's Day and they would perform the marriage ceremony for free. The couples were asked to only purchase the marriage certificate. It was rather pathetic but I was so desperate to be wed before the baby was born that I settled for such a generic wedding. I wanted to do what I thought was best for my unborn child.

Earl had recently undergone chemo-therapy for Non-Hodgkin's Lymphoma so he was unable to make the trip and attend. Mabel flew down to help buy me a few bridal accessories along with a veil.

I remember how I felt when the reception ended up being nothing more than going to McDonald's and taking all the food to a woman's house where we frequently bought our weed. It felt so tacky and cheap and was far less than what I had wanted, expected and deserved.

In April, I began looking into schools I could attend to receive a two year degree. My heart wanted to become a cosmetologist but somehow I became sidetracked and enrolled in a High Secretary course.

I don't know if it was because of the shorter length of time it took in order to obtain a certification, or if it was because the school which I had chosen to attend would hand over the student loan checks directly to you. I started the course in May and by July, I had accumulated about $6000 in cash. I paid for my baby's prenatal care and birth in full.

Rich contributed very little. It was Mabel who helped get the baby's layette and room put together with a crib and bedding set she made for it. After Justin was delivered by cesarean, due to pelvic disproportion, the healing time would require me to take a leave of absence from school. Almost two weeks to the day of his birth, Mabel called and said that Earl was on his deathbed at the hospital and the doctor said I should get there as soon as possible.

I arrived on Wednesday after I flew up with Justin, shortly after Mabel called. After getting settled later that night at Mabel's, she and I went to the hospital to see Earl. I brought Justin along with hopes that Earl would be awake or conscious enough to be able to see his first grandson. When we came to his room, the nurse informed us the visiting hours were almost over and because Earl was so sick, it would not be a good idea to bring a newborn into such a sickly environment. Mabel took Justin downstairs to the cafeteria.

I braced myself, not knowing exactly what I might see. It wasn't all bad but it was far from good. Earl had tubes coming out of everywhere. The one thing that still haunts me to this day is the sound of the ventilator breathing for him. That is a horrible sound, knowing that machine is the only thing keeping someone tied to this earth. I sat there, by his bedside not really knowing what to say.

After the nurses told me that he was pretty much unconscious and heavily sedated, I just sat there. As I looked at him, I felt sorry for this man who lay before me lifeless. I knew his days were diminishing. I still felt hatred towards him for all the hell he put me through and now here he was, dying.

Because I had been on the road for five years, I didn't have very many opportunities to unleash my soul and tell him how angry I was at him. I stood up, not knowing if he would even hear me. I told him that I would write him a long letter. I didn't tell him it was because it was too hard to look at him and think at the same time.

In the next few days, the phone rang constantly with family members showing concern. That was the extent of their communication. I could see more so now that he was the black sheep and never did quite fit into his family either. I believe that is what contributed to his mental illness. Mabel's family wasn't much better; they were even colder with no open displays of love and affection.

It all felt surreal to be back in the house from where only years before, I ran away from. Now, here I am back as an adult and a mother. It was Saturday evening and it felt like the timing was right to begin my letter to Earl. I took Thursday and Friday to gather my thoughts. I drove the old Chevrolet Caprice around to contemplate where I could get away to find some solitude.I remembered a parking area that overlooked the Susquehanna River, after searching aimlessly for the perfect spot as the sun was going down. This place was perfect with the city lights being mirrored on the water.

I borrowed a large legal pad and several different pens while I searched my soul and thought of exactly what I wanted to say. Before I knew it, 2 1/2 hours had passed and I had been writing nonstop. It was now dark. I wanted to be sure to make it to Earl before the nurse sedated him for the night. I also wanted to be able to spend some quality time with him.

When I arrived at the hospital, I went into the chapel and sat for a minute. I didn't pray or beg, I simply felt the need to go in. I then went up to Earl's floor, the ICU. The nurse who was attending him greeted me. I told her about the great letter I wrote and I was hoping that he would be able to acknowledge me as I read it to him. She apologized and said she had just administered the morphine and sedatives and the chances of him hearing me were slim. She encouraged me to try anyway.

I stood there beside his bed and told him I had written and finished the letter I promised to write. I wasn't sure if he could hear me but I wanted to read it to him anyway. The letter was seven pages long, front and back. It felt so good as I read those words, telling him that I forgave him. I told him how much I hated all the horrible things that I was made to deal with as a child because of him.

After the letter was completely read, I leaned in beside him and softly asked, "Did you hear me?" I repeated the question. His lips began opening and closing around the large tube which went down his throat. There was a lot of tape surrounding his mouth, so there was not a lot of space for him to move his lips, but he was trying. He kept moving his mouth until tears were streaming down my face. I laid my head down on his chest and held his hand for a while. I felt so good and had a sense of relief. Visiting hours were long past over.

I told the nurse on my way to the elevator that Earl was trying to communicate emotions and he heard me as I read the letter. She tried to discourage my happiness by saying he was heavily medicated and it was highly unlikely. But I knew that he had. I felt at peace. It was nearly 10 PM when I arrived back home; not 10 minutes had passed after I had walked through the door, when the phone rang. Earl had let go and passed away. I guess he made peace with me too.

ONCE BITTEN TWICE SHY

Not much time went by before I returned back home to Florida. It was in late September when Earl had passed away and I wanted to celebrate the new life of my son with his father, my now husband on my birthday. Of course, when you fight a lot, you make up a lot. On November 12th, the exact same day, I conceived and was pregnant again, at 19. The second due date was merely a few months later. It felt like I was pregnant for two straight years.

By February and the one year supposed anniversary, Rich became very possessive and frightened me when he punched holes in the doors and walls and began to treat me like I was living in a prison. Mabel moved down from Pennsylvania to help us purchase a double-wide mobile home. She did not want to live alone and she wanted to be near when her second grandson was born. I decided I would have Jeremy by Cesarean on her birthday as a genuine gift of love.

The double-wide home we purchased was a brand new 28 x 56, with three bedrooms and two baths. We found a fairly new mobile home park, called the Estates out in the country a little ways north of Gibsonton. Moving that far out was a huge mistake.
Even though Mabel lived with us, I was not permitted to drive her car. I was restricted more or less to the confines of the house and the proximity of the park 24 hours a day.

Unbeknownst to me, I had severe postpartum depression. It began wearing on me mentally to not have anyone to talk to during the day. Rich would come home after screwing off all day, bringing home no money. Mabel would come home from work. He refused to care for Justin and Jeremy and then forced me to drop out of night school.

At night, Mabel would never want to go anywhere. I would plead with Rich to let me drive his van so I could get out of the house for a little time for myself. I needed to have a break from the house and the babies. What made the situation entirely worse is that with Jeremy, Rich's badgering me to have an abortion was relentless all throughout my pregnancy. He let it be known that he only cared about his number one son and number two son was not welcome. He made me stressed out every single day I was pregnant.

Right up to the time that I went into labor, he was still arguing with me on the way to the hospital in the van about some stupid thing. It was so bad and I was so upset, I almost didn't let him into the delivery room with me.

When Jeremy was born by Cesarean as well, I had a very hard time recuperating from the surgery. Caring for an 11-month-old baby and a newborn at the same time was overwhelming because I was in so much physical pain. But that wasn't the point. I needed some sense of self-identity. I was starving for interaction with other people and to be social.

I began to withdraw more and then fell into a worse serious deep depression. Rich finally bought me a junk 1976 Nova for $100 down. He also bought a used washer and dryer, yet the clothes would remain in dirty piles on the laundry room floor until he or Mabel would do it. Dishes would pile up in the sink with baby bottles and sour milk mixed in. I began to resent them for having the freedom to come and go and the more they tried to make me do the housework, the less I did it.

I barely had the mental and physical strength to care for myself and my babies. The only role in life I fulfilled was mother and caregiver. Eventually, I refused to be a wife, maid and cook.Mabel was helpful when it came to paying bills. She had loads of money from Earl's life insurance policy. Rich could never seem to make enough money to support our family as a freelance customizing artist. He refused to get a real job.

Of course, when I brought up the subject of me getting a job, gainful employment was always out of the question. He was too proud or too arrogant to have a wife who wanted to be in the workplace. Mabel always made sure the children were dressed nicely. She took them to Sears to have their pictures taken in similar chosen outfits. Justin was 15 months and Jeremy was only 6 months old by our third anniversary on February 14th.

The date was not acknowledged because a few months earlier around Christmas I had informed Rich that hc would be staying at home with the children while I went in search of a job that day. He threw a fit while shouting at me that he was to not be disrespected and forced to be the homebound, house parent all the way out the door. I still left full of determination to gain some stability for myself and my children. I was willing to walk to the nearest bus stop two miles away, and ready to learn about the mass transit system. I was hired at a tobacco store in the mall.

My second real job allowed me to smoke cigarettes from all over the world. Sobranie Cocktail cigarettes from Russia that have black and rainbow cigarettes with gold filters. Davidoff, a Swiss cigarette and Jakarta clove cigarettes from Indonesia were also part of my favorite expensive vice splurges. I spent so many hours shopping in my brief stripper days and the habit was just as strong now, though restrained for my children.

Over the coming weeks, Rich called the store repeatedly to be disruptive and harass me. He badgered me about having to care for the children. He always included screaming at me that he was the breadwinner. Between Rich and Mabel, who began joining in the destruction of my job, got me fired from too many excessive calls and disrupting the workplace.

When I first mentioned leaving him, Rich faked some health woe by calling an ambulance so I would feel sorry for him and change my mind. It made me hate him even more. I made it to February 23rd and I couldn't take it anymore. I went to the building where Rich rented a stall to work and I told him I was leaving him for good and was going to file for divorce. I wasn't going to take his mental, physical, emotional and controlling abuse any longer.

I informed him I intended to take the children with me but I would stay in Tampa so he could be a part of their lives. If we could put our differences aside for the sake of the children, coparenting to the best of our abilities would be the best. I had the best of intentions. Without blinking an eye he said, "If you leave with my children, I will hunt you down for the rest of your life and kill you, then take my boys! They are my boys! If you don't want me, you don't want them!"

For a brief moment, I had a vision of getting a gun and killing him right where he stood. I was not going to allow him to threaten me or the children ever again. I knew that was not the answer but the protective mama bear emerged and I had never been violent a day in my life. I went back to the house defeated. I sat there all afternoon and pondered about what I was going to do. Reality spoke loud and clear: I had to break free.

In all actuality, I had nowhere to go. I couldn't picture myself out there in the world, living out of the junk car they bought me until I could get an apartment or assistance or anything for that matter.My major concern was my children's welfare. I spoke to Mabel and told her I needed her to help me get out by helping Rich care for the children until I could get a good job and apartment. In all, I had nothing in the world but a piece of crap car with ¼ tank of gas. I asked Mabel for $50, then packed my clothes and waited for Rich to return home.

When he arrived, I met him in the driveway with the car already packed with all my things and informed him that I was leaving, once and for all. He went inside and picked up Justin and Jeremy, bringing them out to me. I continued to get in the car and said, " You have threatened me for the last time. I will be back when I get an apartment – you can take care of the children until then." He started sobbing and said things like, "I will change!" It was too late. Too little, too late.

Too much damage had already been done, especially to my soul. I looked up and saw Mabel standing in the window as I mouthed the words to her,"I'll be back." I had no choice but to trust her and rely on her loyalty to me as her daughter to help me when the time came to move the children out. I envisioned she would get an apartment close to mine and we could have a decent relationship to help the children feel safe and loved.

I also hoped that eventually Rich would lose his anger and hostility to become committed to being a good father by working with me instead of against me and do what was best for our children. He would need to realize they needed the love of both parents. Looking in the rearview mirror as I was pulling out, was the last I saw of my children for a very long time.

As I pulled out onto the highway, I didn't know what I was going to do or where I was going to go but I knew there was no turning back. I felt liberated, as though I knew I was making the right choice for myself and my children. Unknowingly, at this point I also had PTSD. I knew if I lost my mind, I would be no good for them or me. I figured the children were young enough that they could make the transition when the timing was right.

I went to the place where I felt most comfortable, the mall in hopes of contemplating my situation and to secure a job. During my short employment at the tobacco store, I became friends with the manager, Heath. I bought myself a cup of coffee and went to the store to see if he was working. The mall was very desolate during the day which enabled us to talk in between the sparse customers. He offered me a place to live after I told him through tears that I had to leave my children.

He commended me for standing up for myself and my values and understood my heartbreak, leaving my babies. He still had three hours left on his shift, so I made use of the time by filling out applications because I knew I did not want to return to the dancing world. If I got hired, I could catch a ride with him if we could manage to get similar hours. Or I could take the bus. It sounded like a wonderful plan and soothed my bruised and broken soul.

We went out to his very old, ugly car and he gave me a ride to the other side of the mall to get my ugly car, so I could follow him home. He lived in the part of town where low income people and minorities were abundant because rent was super cheap. I couldn't get hired anywhere with no real prior work experience. I think my lack of experience or my lack of self-confidence with no experience doing anything, was showing.

I made many attempts to contact Rich and Mabel to ask how the babies were doing. I always tried to arrange for them to spend time with me. Each and every time I called to talk with Rich, he would fly off the handle for whatever reason. When I went to the house to speak to him directly, he began to refuse to allow me to see my children. I ended up leaving in tears every time.

His psyched out Vietnam Veteran's repeated message to me was,"This Is War- Take No Prisoners."One early evening, I drove down to the mobile home or so called estates so I could pick the boys up at the babysitters before Rich got home. I desperately needed to be with my babies, so she let me into her house. I picked Justin up and held him close to me breathing him in, while peeking at Jeremy sleeping in the bassinet. Before I knew it, a different neighbor along with his wife burst through the door and the man literally pulled Justin from my arms.

The commotion woke Jeremy, who then began to cry so I ran over to pick him up. The other neighbor said, "Rich told us to prevent you from taking the children. He told us to not let you have them if you showed up!" I asked them who the hell they thought they were manhandling me and my babies. He physically pushed me out of the house and told me to come back when Rich got home.

Mabel wouldn't answer the door when I walked down the street to the trailer. I was at the door and windows sobbing, "You are supposed to be my mother! How could you be a part of this?" It was then she told me through a crack in the door, it was payback for all the years I was a run away and for her being placed in the spotlight as an unfit mother. She threatened to call the police, so I left.

I cried and cried and cried. In a few weeks, I was served with divorce papers on the grounds of abandonment of my children, as well as adultery. I didn't know what it all actually meant. Rich filed for divorce at the same time he took the children and went into hiding. In Florida, whoever has physical possession of the children when a divorce is filed, it is that parent who receives primary custody. He had abducted the babies with Mabel's help, after the incident at the babysitter's house.

I could see my children only when he found it convenient to allow me to see them, all the while not knowing where my children were actually living now.

BRINGING ON THE HEARTBREAK

I thought Heath, who was 44, and I were merely friends with benefits at first but dealing with all the trauma pushed me into his arms even more for comfort. He lied and told me he loved me. Two months later, I was pregnant by him. I lived on next to nothing while he would disappear and reappear whenever he felt like it. Then he began to leave me for weeks at a time.

I hated living in that apartment alone because I had already experienced horrible incidents in the short time that I had been there. There was a house in front of my apartment that I had to pass by everyday because the driveway to my apartment went right beside their house. I always noticed a stench emanating out of their house but I never really thought anything about it. I started to briefly talk now and then to the woman who had a husband and two children. I went up to the house one day to borrow something or other and I knocked which then made the unlocked door open a little.

At first, I just poked my head in the door while calling out her name; the smell was even worse inside the house. Then my eyes started to really take notice of what all was before me. I had to walk in a little further to confirm. The bedroom that belonged to the children had a lock on the outside of the door but the door was open. I could definitely see there was feces all over the room.

I was horrified and ran out of the house then called the police and Children and Families. Those children were removed from the house of horrors that afternoon. Being pregnant made my emotions that much more prevalent and definitely much stronger, as my heart broke for those children. I asked myself if my children could be experiencing the same thing? Rich was abusing me. Could he be abusing them too?

The second incident involved the house to my right. The house sat on the corner and the backyard was directly in front of my patio. I would sit on that patio at night usually to cool off. I always noticed that the backyard of the house was super overgrown like a jungle. I figured it was because the house belonged to an old woman; she just didn't care anymore.

One night, as I was sitting there on the patio as the sun was going down, I saw the old woman come out of her back door and had her arms wrapped around a giant dish around 3 inches deep. She walked slowly across the yard to where wires were hanging down from a tree for the dish to be placed in for what I thought was for birds. She stood there when all of a sudden I started to see movement coming from everywhere in every direction and the trees, the bushes and the ground but I couldn't tell what it was at first. To my absolute and ultimate dismay,giant rats were coming out of the garage and everywhere down the trees and down that wire and in that dish while she was standing there.

There were so many rats in the dish that it was bending down from the weight. I was so stunned I didn't know what to say at first. I quickly walked over to the edge of the fence and said, " Ma'am, what are you doing? Why are you feeding rats? You have to get back to your house!" She looked at me and said, "Oh no, they are birds." Again, I called the police and made a report so her daughter could be contacted to deal with the situation appropriately.

In order to eat, I had to apply for food stamps, welfare and shop at food pantries. Mabel started to bring the children to visit when she realized she was going to be a grandmother again. I thought we were beginning to mend our relationship but why then I don't know. I was very grateful for her trying to do the right thing for all of us. She confided to me that she was beginning to question Rich's actions and motives.

She insisted that she had to have them back on time, for fear of what he would do to her if she was late or if he found out she brought them to visit. Every time I buckled the boys into the car seats and kissed them goodbye, I felt like my heart was being ripped out. I tried not to cry in front of them but it was hard. Mabel began to come by and would purchase groceries and hygiene items that I needed. I guess she felt sorry for me, suffering as badly as I was as I was getting more pregnant by the day with an absentee father nowhere in sight.

Throughout the court proceedings of the divorce and child custody, I was made to look more and more like a fool because I had no clue how to represent myself. Tragically, had I known the legal ramifications of statutory rape at that time, I could have shown how corrupt he was and I would never had to be separated and kept from my babies. Rich hired one of the best attorneys in Tampa. I could not afford an attorney. I foolishly believed from my brief education experiences that if I told the truth, justice would prevail.

I knew in my heart I had done nothing wrong. I thought for sure the judge would at least allow the children to live with me and give the two of us joint custody. He did not do that, in fact he gave Rich sole custody. After months of numerous battles with Rich and taking him back to court for not allowing me to have my designated time for visits with the children, the judge hardly slapped him on the wrist and instructed him only to be more cooperative. All the while Heath kept leaving me so I ended up turning back to dancing when I was four months pregnant. I couldn't survive without money any longer and Mabel's support was dwindling in every way.

I would be up on stage telling the men I was pregnant not fat! Here I was again, back at the ground-zero slum club. Oddly, for some men pregnancy was a major turn on. My breasts were getting bigger everyday for sure, along with my growing belly. Every afternoon I would take the bus across town to work at Fantasy's; it was the only dive bar that I was pretty sure would accept my belly as long as I could dance.

I performed until I was nearly 8 months along, but then I had to stop, for obvious reasons. I managed to pay the rent and live a semi-decent life while I bought clothing and other things at thrift stores for the baby who was soon to come. Heath finally reconciled with his responsibility that he was about to be a father shortly before my due date. He came to the apartment and helped me pack, then took me with him over to his mother's house in Clearwater, across the bay from Tampa.

He said he had been staying at her house most of the time he was missing and he used the custody battle for my children as a lame excuse for his absence. His mother hated me and I was not welcome in her home so I sat in the car. Heath was definitely a rotten mama's boy but he was attempting to defy her and be true to me. I was happy to be out of the hellish apartment and willing to deal with whatever I had to. Heath's mom ended up giving him money for us to stay at a motel while he sorted out the final details for an apartment.

He found a motel for us located just outside of town.
I think maybe he had a woman stashed somewhere so he put me way out, nearly into the next town for a reason. It was next to the water so when I would walk up to the convenience store, on the water's edge while I stopped to think and pray that everything, somehow, would work itself out for the best. After two weeks of residing at the motel, Heath came back to the room one afternoon and told me he was leaving for good. I began screaming from complete fear of being abandoned in a town I did not know. I jumped into his car after him and pleaded with him to not abandon me again. I couldn't fight or deal with all of it anymore.

My heart was breaking more and more with each passing day because my arms ached to hold my children yet I was forbidden to be a part of Justin and Jeremy's lives. I didn't think I could get through this pregnancy and birth alone. I had nowhere to go or stay. I was terrified. He callously threw me out of his car and then he was gone.

What I did next will confirm just how depressed I had become. I took an entire bottle of Tylenol in a weak attempt to kill myself and inadvertently my unborn child. I simply could not go on anymore. It felt as though I had no fight left in me, but I did. I called an ambulance and told them what I had done. I was rushed to the hospital and my stomach was forcibly pumped to get the Tylenol out of my system.

I was relieved to be told after I woke up with a tube down my nose that I didn't hurt my baby. I was more ashamed and heartbroken over my actions than anything. The mental health staff came up to the intensive care unit to talk with me. After explaining all of my current circumstances and past experiences in my life, the woman realized I wasn't a threat to myself or others. I was simply traumatized, overstressed and extremely depressed. She provided me with a list of resources and contacts for after I was able to be released.

ESTRANGED

Later that day, there was a phone call that came into the nurses station. It was a man saying that he was concerned and would like to know when I was to be released so he could come to pick me up. He explained that he was friends with the motel owner and found out that I was no longer welcome there, so he had all my belongings. He offered that I could stay at his house for as long as I needed, because he lived alone. He also mentioned he was a paraplegic who used a wheelchair but could drive to pick me up.

Upon entering his home, he showed me to my room and how to adjust the heat because it got cold and damp at night. The following day was uneventful until nightfall, when all hell broke loose. I don't know if it was alcohol or drug-induced, or if he was just flat out psychotic. He turned into a madman and chased me around his house in his wheelchair with a butcher knife! I made my way to the bedroom and locked the door, then moved the heavy dresser in front of it.

As pregnant as I was, I shouldn't have been moving heavy furniture but I thought I was going to die and was shaking uncontrollably from adrenaline and fear, which gave me amazing strength. I sat against that dresser the entire night almost until dawn with him pounding on the door saying things like, "You got to come out sometime bitch!" I kept asking, "Why are you doing this to me?" He stopped the madness and the house was quiet and still around 4 AM. I sat quietly waiting to find the moment to escape.

I gathered my most important belongings and moved the dresser quietly away from the door. I wasn't sure if he was just outside the door or not. I made my way out towards the front door with no sign of him. In a moment I was safely out on the sidewalk. I started walking fast, never looking back at the house. I could not believe how strange and terrifying life was becoming around every bend in the road. I knew I had to be brave for my children and I reminded myself of how I had already come so far with life.

I walked up to the corner convenience store and pulled out the list of resources I was given at the hospital. I asked to use their phone and decided to call the local battered women's shelter. I was asked a few qualifying intake questions and was then advised to call a cab which she would pay for when I arrived. I stayed at the shelter for two weeks before I went in search of Heath. The baby was just about to be born.

I was on welfare so I was not permitted to have a cesarean birth as I did previously, twice before. No, this child was to be born as a VBAC- vaginal birth after Cesarean. I was concerned about my pelvic disproportion.

The day I went into labor it was early morning on May 2nd. I walked myself to the hospital located nearly 20 blocks away. When I arrived, they checked my cervix and I was not dilated enough so therefore, I would need to come back in a few hours. There was no way I could walk all that way again. In a very nice way I said, "Give me some Pitocin or whatever you've got to give me and I'll walk some more but I'm not leaving this hospital!"

They gave into my demands and I was admitted into Labor and Delivery. I tried to call Mabel who started being more civil to me to let her know I was in labor. I was determined to get through this new experience of natural childbirth though I was given many Darvon to help with the pain. When my third baby boy was born, he was laid on the warming table and put his little hand up to his face without crying at first, as he checked out the bright, new world around him. Mabel arrived three hours after he was born.

I couldn't wait to name him but for the life of me, I couldn't come up with a suitable name. A book I was reading helped me choose it: Matthias. There was no stable income coming in other than my welfare check so I made my rounds each and every week to the local food pantries. There was an agency which gave out vouchers to a Publix grocery store which was the closest to me. My spirits were very low one particular evening, alone with my baby.

I received a voucher earlier in the day so I got Matthias situated comfortably in his stroller and set out for the walk to the store. The voucher I received entitled the recipient to hygiene products and necessities such as toilet paper as well as food. As I made my way through the aisles when I came to the bread department something inside me told me to grab an extra loaf. After checking out, I put my groceries in the stroller and carried Matthias in my arms.

Upon crossing the street, a man approached me out of nowhere. It was dark by then so I was a little startled. He asked if I had any food I could spare, after explaining he was a homeless Vietnam Veteran, down on his luck. I told him the only extra food I could offer was a loaf of bread. He was grateful and thanked me. As I turned around to continue on my way, guilt set in knowing that I could've given him the package of baloney I had purchased.

I could not have taken more than 10 steps when I turned back around and he was gone. The man had completely disappeared and vanished. I walked the rest of the way home wondering if angels really do exist. I also wondered if I just passed some sort of test. So near to Christmas, perhaps I had experienced a miracle.

I called the women's shelter I stayed at previously and asked if I could have lodging and assistance with childcare while I began to look for work. They told me I was welcome to reside there again. Matthias was nearly 3 months old by this time. I did manage to get a small part-time job and could work while the other women would watch Matthias for me without charge, which was a definite blessing.

I was at the shelter for nearly 3 weeks when Rich said I could have visits with Justin and Jeremy 1 who were now two and three years old. In order to make this happen I had to ride the bus, which was no easy task with three small children. To get from Clearwater to Tampa, I had to ride seven different buses which were on a strict schedule. I had to make sure I was on time at each stop or a mistake could mess up the entire trip. I started out at five in the morning and did not arrive with the children, back at the shelter until around six at night.

I thought Rich would have helped make it a little easier for me, but no, this was part of his take no prisoners motto because to him this was a war. I was permitted to see my children only when it was convenient for him or he had something to do. On the second visit, upon returning back to the shelter, Justin said he had to use the potty, so I took him. As I helped him with his pants and underwear, I noticed that his scrotum was very bruised.

I gently asked Justin what had happened. He said, "Somebody kicked me." I then asked him, "What? Who? Who baby? Who kicked you?" He kept saying that he wasn't supposed to tell. I internally went ballistic, having difficulty in trying to contain my emotions. I asked the shelter director how I should handle it. She said to be patient and keep asking questions in different ways until one or both children would confide who exactly kicked him.

That same afternoon, I discovered that both of my babies had lice so I applied for medicinal treatment. The boys were not enrolled in daycare so the lice had to come from within the home. That infuriated me even more. My son's were both happy with their new little brother Matthias and we took lots of pictures while we enjoyed our time together.

I continued trying to get the truth of the injury. I could tell they believed they would be punished if they told. Out of the blue during dinner, Jeremy said, "Daddy hurt Justin." I then asked Justin, "Is that right? Did Daddy kick you?" He said yes.
That was it. While they were down for their nap, I called the police and child protection services, with the support of the director.

The police interrogated the children for hours, which I felt was very unprofessional. They were both terrified they were going to get their father into trouble by doing something wrong and telling them. After a while, when the questions were asked in so many different combinations, the boys withdrew and wouldn't answer any more questions. I was appalled at the policeman so I asked him, "Do you not see that they are only just babies, protecting their father?" You handled this entire situation all wrong.

Their findings stated there was not enough evidence as proof of abuse. Rich had a contract with the Hillsborough County Sheriff's Office to do painting on their vehicles; I knew that's why justice once again, did not prevail. I was inconsolable. I then called Rich myself and told him the children would not be returning to live with him.

I didn't care what the court paperwork said. Within days, the sheriff's deputy came to the shelter and took Justin and Jeremy away. I then had to appear in court, where trying to protect my babies, got me found in contempt of court. The judge was going to make me serve 30 days in county jail. I explained that I had no one to care for Matthias so he let me go.

I stayed at the shelter for several more weeks. Near the end of my stay, Matthias had a very high fever and was screaming in pain when I had to change his diaper. I took him to the hospital. After a spinal tap was performed, the doctors concluded that he had contracted viral meningitis. I could only guess that he contracted it from the shelter, I just didn't know.

It was at this point in my life when I started slipping backwards into the downward slide of depression. Matthias was hospitalized for about a week. Mabel came and visited more often after he was released. I spent my days ahead passing time by walking with him around Clearwater in the stroller. I was trying to get myself back into shape so I could go back to dancing to support myself and have a fighting chance to get my children back.

When he was eight months old, he began learning to walk. One day Matthias was standing on the outside of his walker, holding on and pushing it. Within the fraction of a split second, he sped up and fell into the space heater. I quickly scooped him up and ran with him cradled in my arms, down to the hotel on the corner because I didn't have a phone. I asked them to call 911. The burn was bad but thankfully it did not leave a bad scar.

I felt like I was going to lose it. I was beginning to question my abilities as a mother and human being? How could this accident have happened? I should not have let him push the walker. He sped up so fast that there was not enough reaction time for me to have prevented it but I let him push it and that was a bad decision.

I borrowed $100 from Mabel to pay for a weeklong stay at Motel 6 over in Tampa, so I could dance.I managed to find a babysitter who would watch Matthias from nine at night to five in the morning, the hours I was working at the club. After a few nights of working at the not so busy club, I found that my body image and self-confidence was super low and it was getting the best of me. I decided to try out lingerie modeling for a while instead of dancing. I saw an ad in the paper and called the contact number. I asked the man what was exactly involved with being a lingerie model.

He explained the job was for a brand new shop and I would be modeling lingerie for customers. After choosing which piece they liked the most, I was to encourage them to make their purchase. The man on the phone assured me that I could make at least $100 each day. It wasn't great money but it would pay the bills and room rent until I could raise my confidence level and go back to exotic dancing.

Matthias was already at the sitters that night so I asked her if she could keep him through the next day. I would then pick him up later that night. She said it would be ok. I arrived at the lingerie shop at 2 pm and I sat there all day with not one single customer coming through the door. By 10pm that night I was mad. He then suggested if I would be willing to pull some tricks, he could hook me up with some good clientele. I was so angry because I wasted my entire day on his lies.

The shop was merely a front for prostitution. I had to pay the babysitter and feed my son! I could have danced but now it was too late. I went to the back room to get dressed and gather my things. I had been wearing nothing but a piece of lingerie all day long. I walked my way back up to the front of the store and on the couch just inside the door, lay a small Derringer pistol. This made me even more upset. Any fool might have walked in through that door and the situation could have turned ugly. I picked up the gun and put it in my bag.

As I made the long walk back to the motel with no cab fare I was trying to think of what I was going to do, after I called the sitter and explained the situation.A few hours later, well after midnight the man from the store was pounding on my door and demanding his gun back. I didn't answer him so he eventually left. The next day I walked for an hour to get to a gun pawn shop, where I sold it for $40, using my real name. Not a smart idea. I took the money though and paid the babysitter and bought Matthias some formula and diapers.

That same night I went to a mediocre club, Lipstixx. I figured with a flabby body or not this was a slow enough club that I shouldn't get judged too harshly for my flaws. I couldn't wait to get myself back into hard body shape again so I would be able to work at a high-class-high-volume-high-dollar club where the elite clientele would be. I made an acquaintance that night with a man who on every subsequent visit to the club, would bring me what he called a "care package." Each and every night I danced, within each tinfoil care package, there would be a little cocaine, a few joints, a few Valium, Dilaudid and even morphine from time to time.

The different colored lights pulsating to the music so loud you could feel it through your bones. With cigarette smoke heavy in the air and the smoke machine going too, made it feel even more out of this world. I felt so much power as I gave away every ounce of energy I had to a roaring crowd. The haze in the air matched the haze in my head. I never sought out help for my depression so I believe I began to self- medicate in hopes of feeling better.

I began drinking a lot of alcohol around this time too. It did not take much time for me to become a fall-down stumbling drunk. Between the drugs and booze, I was trashed every morning when I picked Matthias up from the babysitter's. It grew harder and harder for me to care for him because he would be wide awake all day while I was dealing with my head pounding hangovers, he would be in his crib for hours some days. I merely wanted to sleep off all the effects of partying too hard.

GIRLS, GIRLS, GIRLS

I moved into a brand new apartment, in a newly built complex with an awesome move-in special that secured the place next to nothing. The complex was modern and just built with a pool a little ways from my door, located in the center of the courtyard. Some afternoons, I would take Matthias out and we would sit by the edge of the pool with the other mothers and children. After living there for a few months, I switched the club I was working at to work at a more upscale club that was pretty close by.

I tried to spend quality time with Matthias and being a good mom, it simply felt like it was not enough. I was failing again, as a human being and as a mother. Even though I paid the sitter well, she could see what a train wreck I was becoming but held her tongue time and time again. The Tanga Lounge was my new club and had an in-house make-up artist and hairstylist to help us get more beautiful. It was here that I changed my stage name to Midnight. When people would ask, "Why Midnight?" I would tell everyone the same thing every time, "Everyone has a dark side."

The previous club I worked at, 2001 Odyssey was decent but most of the nightly business was slower due to a popular club across the street, the Mons Venus. The owner JR, is considered the father of the nude lap dance so we all owe him some due credit. The Mons is packed to capacity every night of the week. At the time I didn't like the way they handled the girls and I definitely did not like sharing a small stage with four other dancers. I learned that the stage belonged to me when it was my turn to be up and there was no room for anyone else under the spotlights.

The unique aspect of the 2001 Odyssey strip club is it has a round-shaped spaceship in which you and your customer ascend a steep flight of stairs to perform private dances for him. It was quirky but I could always lure a man up there with a description of the dance room to the inside of the bottle on the TV show, I Dream of Jeannie. The layout was remarkably similar. One particular afternoon I showed up early, around three. There was hardly any clientele at that time so I sat in the back, leisurely getting myself ready to perform. The costume lady showed up so I had her and the costume racks all to myself.

I took the time to try on several different pieces. I had been predominantly wearing a white lace teddy thing and I was getting really bored with it. I only had $60, so my selections were very limited. I came across a black velvet one piece G-string that fit me like a glove.
The DJ came back to the dressing room to give me heads up. The customers were starting to filter in so being first, I needed to get out onto the floor and mingle. Wearing my new simple outfit, full of renewed confidence, I stepped out from behind the curtain onto the stage. There were a few men sitting at the bar.

One man walked over to sit closer at the stage to watch me dance. That man ended up giving me 4 dances for $100, 14 times, later that evening. It amazed me how a simple change of outfit could change my attitude enough to instantly attract like that. I walked out a very happy dancer that night, amazed how everything changed in a matter of minutes. I switched clubs again and this time, I decided for notoriety I would take a limousine every day to and from work, instead of a cab. My daily fare went from $6 to $70!

I became friends with the manager of the limo company so I received good deals and was allowed to have my favorite driver who was from Persia. His name was Ruiz and he was sexy and hot! We would have crazy sex in the back of the limo in different settings after I got off of work which was exceptionally erotic. My friend from the limo company called one afternoon and told me he had a potentially lucrative proposition for me. He explained that he had a friend who was sentenced to prison in New York for a very long time.

He made hints that this man was a part of some Mafia family, but didn't share too many details. The family needed me to do a few harmless things that could possibly help this man get out of prison. He asked if I would be willing to help. I apprehensively said that I would help the cause. My associate gave the man's mother my home phone number. When she called, she explained what exactly was wanted from me. She needed me to snap a few Polaroid pictures of a dancer with whom I worked with.

Somehow the dancer caused serious trouble with lies and deception, which resulted in the man's long prison term. She was not supposed to be in the vicinity or working in any club, the reason was unclear. My job sounded easy enough. I was told the mother would Overnight Mail me $250 money order the next day in good faith to seal the deal with more or less, front money. When I completed the task and produced the pictures, I would then be paid $5,000 cash, with no questions asked.

The next day the money arrived as promised. I went and bought the camera then waited a few nights for the right opportunity to snap a few shots of the girl.
Every night before work when Ruiz would pick me up for work, I would have him cruise me across the Courtney Campbell Causeway to cover a few miles crossing the bay while I listened to songs like November Rain over and over again. I always had a bottle of whiskey stashed in my dance bag, along with plenty of joints. I would have the stereo blasting as I mentally prepared myself to deal with idiots and jerks that I would have to deal with later that night at work.

It always felt great, pulling up to the club in my long, black limousine. There was a Mexican Cantina next to the club then beyond the restaurant was a small bar where I began spending obscene amounts of money before every shift buying White Russians, my drink of choice at the time. I became good friends with two girls that I danced and worked with, Sky and Raven. I would bring them along in the limo sometimes before work so we could drive Ruiz wild as we partied, giving him his own little show from the rearview mirror while he drove us around.

Sometimes, he couldn't take it and had to pull over, climb in the back and join in. It was so much fun. My two friends and I always went over to the

Cantina for our first break. One night, as we exited the club, we couldn't help but notice there were two official looking guys in black suits talking to our boss in front of the club. They stopped talking for a minute when we passed by them. We didn't really think anything of it. The girls and I went into the Cantina, which was always very busy through the dinner hour and found some seats at the bar. We ordered our drinks and appetizers.

Out of nowhere, a man came right up behind me and said, "Excuse me, are you Midnight?" Without turning around, thinking it was a customer who followed us over, I asked, "Who wants to know?"
He replied, "FBI, can I have a word with you?" What the hell? It turned out, the phone belonging to the mother of the man who was in prison in upstate New York, had been tapped. Every phone call and every phone that had been used in connection with him and her were listened to and monitored by the Feds.

The agent asked if we could sit at a table and talk. Raven and Sky looked at me puzzled and wide-eyed as they remained seated at the bar. The Federal Agent went on to tell me that they were aware of exactly what my involvement had been so far and the amount of money I had been offered for the deal.

Then he said, "We will double their offer and pay you $10,000, if you don't help them." I sat there for a minute, trying to think fast. The only words that came out were, "Fuck all of this! I don't want any part of this with you or them! Don't worry about me, I want no part of this." I casually went back to work as my break had long since been over, feeling a little spooked.

By now, my body was ready to work in any club I set my mind to like The Dollhouse. The temptation to make extra fast money kept arising because a lot of other dancers had a very lucrative side hustle. A Hilton Hotel was across the highway and the majority of men that came into our club were businessmen from out of town and were always looking for company. It was hard to resist the temptation of easy money.

Usually, for an hour or so, the going rate was $300 or more depending on what the man wanted. The problem was, I vowed I would never sell my body again now that I could take men's money without losing my dignity. I did not want to even acknowledge all the times in the past that I had no other choice. I felt like I was reclaiming my body.

Between the short, spiky hair and the forever worn black leather thigh-high boots, I began to attract men who appreciated a dominatrix. I ran with that concept and acquired the props and a lot more leather outfits to entice the fantasy even further.

During a private dance, I would be asked to hit, scratch and be wicked to the customers. It was always the men who were in the most powerful positions in America, usually CEOs and such. I didn't mind giving them the fantasy while I assisted to bring them down a few notches.

One night, another dancer and I were called over to a table where five men were sitting. They looked as though they were from Saudi Arabia, with a dark foreign look. They would pay each of us $1,000 to fulfill a fantasy that one of the men had. The men only wanted to watch; the request was made for their friend. We were curious but had heard stories of how violent some foreign men could be, but this group seemed harmless enough; only deprived of having their wildest fantasies fulfilled. We had to make a quick trip to the sex store before we went to the hotel room.

The man's request was to watch the other dancer and I take turns wearing a strap on dick and fucking each other while they watched. There was no participation from them, as promised. It was very kinky and definitely a new experience. It was something that neither her nor I had ever done, or even thought about really.

I was a little uncomfortable, but I think only because I was a bit nervous. It all went well and when it was over as promised, they gave us $1000 each, then we called a cab and left. It was a strange experience, I have to admit. It's a good thing I was trashed because I was pretty sure I didn't like it and would never do it again.

NO MORE TEARS

I kept screwing up, getting too messed up and I began to leave Matthias for days at a time at the babysitters. She seemed to be understanding but it turned out that her husband was making it very hard on her to be unbiased towards my behavior. He insisted she should turn me into the Department of Children and Families. She tried to make excuses for me as long as she could. After all, I was paying her very well, sometimes over $200 each night.

It got to the point where partying all night at the club just wasn't enough anymore. I began going to after hour bars till sunup, after my club closed at 4 am. I was entirely wasted one night after my shift so I caught a ride home with some guy and we had stopped at an intersection for a red light. I thought I was going to puke so I opened the door and leaned out, then failed to close it right. As he proceeded to make a left turn, I fell out of the car, rolled a few times and got a major road rash while ruining a pair of brand new leather shorts. Thank goodness it happened in the middle of the night, with no traffic.

I met an Asian man somewhere along the way who owned a prominent restaurant somewhere in town. He would come over once a week and we would have sex. He was very efficient, going so far as to make a schedule for me to follow because there were times when he could squeeze in two or three visits per week. Our appointments lasted no longer than 30 minutes. I made $100 each time he visited.

I always used a condom with all men except on the rare occasion when I would have a boyfriend which was not very often. During this time period, I learned there was a warrant for my arrest. The gun that I had pawned had caught up with me at last: Grand Larceny of a Firearm.

The news sent me into a complete tailspin and the first of many more incidents of self-destruction were to follow. Much worse than where I already had been. I knew I was falling into the deep end and hopelessly drowning. Rich moved far away somewhere with Justin and Jeremy. Mabel refused to tell me where they were now and she still acted like she was afraid of him, though I still didn't know why.

I rented a new motel room after a few days off and took Matthias to the sitter so I could get back to work at the club. I told her I was considering putting my son into temporary foster care. Along with the newly discovered warrant for my arrest still hanging over my head, I realized that my life was out of control. I was a fast moving train headed down the wrong track and on the verge of crashing at any moment.

Instead of getting ready for work, I called the Department of Children and Families myself around 3 o'clock in the afternoon. I did my best to explain my situation and I made sure the woman I was talking to knew that I only wanted to place Matthias in the system for a short amount of time. I would clean up my act and become sober then find another decent place to live due to losing my nice apartment from failure to pay my rent on time.

By 6 pm, a social caseworker went to the babysitters and picked up my only child I had left to love. I knew the babysitter must have made a call too. Matthias was gone. He was better off for the time being, I told myself. I set the proverbial ball in motion to get better. First I cried and I was angry but in my heart I knew it was for Matthias's best interest. I needed to get my shit together.

I ended up staying at Mabel's new apartment for a few weeks because I had no other place to go. I no longer had the means to support myself. I wanted to get a real, respectable job that allowed me to keep my clothes on. I didn't want to be a stripper/hooker anymore. I decided the best thing I could do for starters was to turn myself in for the warrant. There were two jails in Tampa.

I took four hits of acid before going to the downtown police department. I walked into the reception area and before the effects of the LSD really kicked in, I stated my reasons for turning myself in. An officer came through a locked door after a lengthy wait to tell me I was at the wrong jail. I was really beginning to trip hard now. My friends were still outside in the car tripping too, waiting to see if I came out or not. An officer took me to the Orient Road Jail where as I sat there waiting to be officially booked in, I watched the floor breathe.

In the weeks ahead, I tried to do everything that the caseworker requested of me for Matthias. It was all so very hard. I couldn't help feeling like I was predestined to fail, which I did miserably. So I stopped trying and I gave up. I couldn't fight with anyone, anymore for anything.

I had been in jail for a little over a month when the caseworker came for an actual visit and told me that Matthias was being placed for adoption. My heart broke right in two. My hope for redeeming myself was once again shattered. The caseworker told me she thought the placement would be best for him. The foster family he was living with temporarily wanted him to live with them permanently.

They were an older couple who could not have children. Each time I saw pictures of Matthias, he looked happy and healthy. Somewhere deep in my heart I knew this was right, although signing those adoption papers was the hardest thing I had ever done. It felt like my heart had been completely ripped out.

The caseworker assured me as soon as I was released from jail, I could go to the downtown office and put together a file which would have my picture and whatever information I wanted Matthias to know about me for when he turned 18. I think I was in a state of shock for a few days and was a complete basket case. I continued to be detained for the charge of Grand Theft, Larceny of a Firearm. It was my first charge ever and the jails were overcrowded. I was released with a Personal Recognizance bond and was ordered to participate in Pretrial Intervention.

If I followed through with the program, the charge would be completely erased off of my record. I wasn't sure how that was going to go. I went downtown to the caseworker's office to handle the final paperwork for the adoption by completely signing away my parental rights. I brought several photos of myself with Justin and Jeremy and pictures of the four of us together. I then created a file, which included writings of my thoughts and things I wanted Matthias to know about me. The description of me read: Your mom loves Harley Davidson's, nature and cosmetology.

As the caseworker took the file from me, I couldn't help but wonder why my own mother didn't include some type of message for me with my adoption. It was comforting to think that someday Matthias may open that file. After I left her office that day, I went completely wild and I didn't care about anything, anymore. My heart hurt so bad that it felt like it didn't even want to keep on beating. My life became somewhat of a blur after that, as I desperately wasted away on all the drugs and alcohol. I was drowning in sorrow and depression over the loss of my children.

KICKSTART MY HEART

1993 was the year my life started coming back into focus. I ended up going out to Daytona on a Greyhound bus with a $20 ticket. It was the first time I had been back to the town since I was stranded as a teenager, all those years before. I worked at Molly Brown's, a club on Seabreeze Avenue. I simply felt drawn to that club because it reminded me of a club I might see in New York City. I would convince a guy to purchase a bottle of champagne, from which I would receive a percentage at the end of the night.

A bottle of Dom Perignon would give a dancer $48 as a cut, in addition to what I made from the private dances. By the end of the night, I corked the bottle with my tongue and only pretended to drink so the customer would get super drunk. At this time in my exotic dancing career, money was excellent. I was making over $1000 every single night. It was Race Week for the Daytona 500. By the time the week was over I was fired up and ready for Bike Week.

I didn't even want to work, I only wanted to party and ride as many Harleys as I could. The Iron Horse Saloon, Boot Hill Saloon and The Cabbage Patch were my favorite hotspot hangouts. I did switch bars to the Shark Lounge. Dancers performed on a stage that was on top of a very large aquarium that held a shark. At the Shark, I could find the real bikers who had to take their colors off (club patches) at the door before entering. The rest of the strip club bars in Daytona were filled mostly with weekend warriors and fair weather riders. Not my cup of tea.

I have ridden on the back of a motorcycle up north on New Year's Day, needing to wrap Saran wrap around my legs under my jeans to keep the cold out. I later got a full leather set with a feminine, tight fitting vest full of patches and a thick motorcycle coat with a huge Harley-Davidson patch near my lower back, along with chaps and a half helmet full of stickers that said things like D.I.L.L.I.G.A.F. (Does It Look Like I Give A Fuck) and S.N.A.F.U. (Situation Normal All Fucked Up) for my Lid.

There have been many times that I was on the back of a bike and a massive thunderstorm rolled in. Rain hurts when you're going at a different decent speed but you gotta keep going to get through it. My money started going down so I decided to pitch a tent at a campground, on the edge of town, on the mainland side. It was nice to feel secluded and tucked away from the hustle and bustle. The campground would host fun events which went on throughout the week, miles away from all the chaos going over at Daytona Beach.

The campground had a bikini contest so I decided to enter. Just like when I competed in the Miss Boot Hill contest I knew I was not going to win, yet I still had a great time competing. As I was making my way around the crowd strutting my stuff, my eyes locked onto one of the most handsome bikers I had ever seen. We were fixated on each other as the rounds went on. I was able to keep my composure and I actually ended up placing third in the contest.

He then walked over to where I was standing with the other contestants and introduced himself as Dane. He was from Easton, Pennsylvania. I went back to my tent, grabbed a sexy outfit then headed to the bathhouse to glam up. Dane asked me to go for a ride on his cream colored 1979 FLH Harley Davidson, which was dressed out to make it look much older than it was. It was such a beautiful bike.

We rode around for the rest of the day until nearly dusk. Dane told his friends that had accompanied him down to Florida that he was going to be spending most of his time with me for the remainder of their trip and I would be joining them for the ride home. The idea of leaving Florida sounded like a dream. I lost all hope of doing anything else to reverse the damage that had been done in my life. Also, the fact that Mabel finally confessed to me again that she helped Rich steal my children as a punishment for humiliating her and Earl years before, when I was a runaway.

Her treachery didn't make my decision to leave Florida hard at all. I had nothing but contempt in my heart for her and she meant nothing to me anymore. In fact she did not even exist. The ride North on Interstate 95 to Pennsylvania was filled with laughter and most of the time I was sitting on Danes lap because the van we were traveling in was a bit cramped with me as an extra passenger.

No one seemed to mind except for the woman who thought she was going to get Dane to be with her since they were away from their hometown, but she was sadly disappointed. I think he knew her intentions from the start and because of his genuine dislike for her, he rubbed it in by making it well known just how happy he was with me.

After we got settled in Pennsylvania I began looking for work at a bar. In most small towns, the taverns would convert to a Go-Go bar a few times a week or month to attract extra customers and to increase business. The tactic usually worked and it was now almost hunting season so the bars would be filled to the max. Dane would play pool while I was up on stage and working the floor.

I noticed an older man in his late 60s, sitting directly in front of me at the bar. Clearly, I had his full attention. I could tell by the way he was dressed that he was loaded. He came up to the stage and tipped me a $50 bill. He introduced himself as Isaac and as I chatted with him between my songs, I kept looking over at Dane who was looking at me.

The wheels started to turn as I decided right then and there, I was going to make my first Sugar Daddy a reality. I asked the gentleman to buy me a drink for me to join him when I got down off the stage all hot and sweaty. As we sat and talked, I was constructing a storyline to hook my big catch. Dane was gentle, but overall a scary looking biker. I decided the story I was going to run with entailed me pointing to Dane, while telling Isaac, if I did not pay Dane $500, he was going to do terrible things to me.

With biker law, he owned me and I owed him money. He was here at the bar to make sure I paid up. Looking at him, any ordinary man would've been frightened, so the story was not hard to believe. He turned out to be a local veterinarian, who had been in practice for the past 40 years. He was such a sweet man but all I could see were dollar signs.

He gave me both his phone number and clinic phone number, then told me to call him the next day. The following day he took me to lunch and gave me $500.00. With the money in hand, Dane and I decided to take a road trip back down the East Coast and to Florida. This time we headed South, straight to Key West. The entire drive down I was calling Isaac, telling him that Dane had kidnapped me and he was going to sell me in Stone Mountain Georgia, if I didn't do everything he said.

Isaac sent me a few hundred dollars at a time in increments throughout the trip which I would pick up through Western Union, every few towns. I felt a little guilty and cruel but at the same time, brilliant. Before long, there we were laying on the beach in Key West, leaving our worries and worries behind along with the cold of winter, in the middle of March. It was paradise. We watched the sunset celebration and walked through the town arm in arm, going in and out of all the bars.

The beautiful historic homes captivated me as we walked along the side streets and neighborhood.
It was a 5 star all-expenses paid vacation. We stayed for a few days in Key West before heading back up North. I did look into all the clubs in the area but I really did not want to work.

Shortly after we returned, Dane and I eventually split up. Along with my newfound experience of extortion, I discovered that I had acquired and spent around $24,000 from Isaac in that first year. I spent it all on lavish things and living large and I even drove a new Cadillac that had previously been Isaac's ex-wife. It was mine now. By the end of the time that Isaac was a part of my life, the total amount of money that he gave me totaled around $83,000.

In the years ahead, I traveled continuously non-stop all over the country while working in different clubs in different towns. I loved waking up and seeing a new sunrise in a new town. Even though I worked well into the night, I always still got up early for a few hours. I was always content settling in South Dakota for the summer to dance a little but mostly take a break from dancing and work as a waitress in one of the many restaurants in the town of Keystone, Pennsylvania in autumn, part of winter and then down to Florida in early spring.

Each year after I worked faithfully in each state, on my circuit. One year in Daytona, with my new boyfriend, the season ran out and we were short on cash. I knew a guy named Troy, from whom I would buy my weed from. I also knew that Troy always carried around $3,000 in his pocket at any given time. My boyfriend came up with the idea that we roll him.

At first, I wasn't sure exactly what the process was and I was not, and never would be a violent person. I had never violently harmed a living soul in my life, and I didn't intend to start now. My boyfriend convinced me that my only role would be to lure Troy into the apartment, then he would take over and do the rest. He told me he would only hit Troy a few times until he gave up the money.

When I went to Troy's apartment, he had a pound of weed to deliver so I had to wait. I tried to get in before he made the delivery, to make a big score with weed too, but he wanted to get rid of it. I was so scared – for me and more for him. I had never done anything like this before. Troy and I were walking back into the apartment when my boyfriend jumped out of the shadows and started to beat Troy with a pipe.

I ran out and ducked into the laundry room, where I crouched down in the corner, while covering my ears because I could hear what was happening. Troy wasn't giving up his money. What ended up being 20 minutes, seemed like hours. My boyfriend finally came running out into the parking lot, covered with blood, yelling for me. I ran out and said, "Oh My God! You didn't kill him did you?" He assured me that he didn't, but we really needed to find a place to hide. He got the money.

We ran for at least five blocks to the hotels on the beach. When we emerged onto the strip, the Days Inn was right in front of us so that ended up being the chosen hideout. I was shaking almost uncontrollably as I went to the front desk to check in and get the room key. As we went into the room, I ran to the bathroom and puked from adrenaline and fright. I couldn't believe what I had just done. I didn't even think about what my boyfriend had just done.

I asked myself how I could have let my life get to this point. Only weeks before, I had been entertaining a very prominent race car driver's manager, in his condo. My boyfriend and I stayed in that hotel room for a few hours, then we called a taxi. We were headed for Orlando so we had the cab driver take us to the Orlando airport. It was a few hundred dollars fare.

We had no idea what we were going to do or where we were going. We got a room at the Hyatt, located at the airport for two days. The room was over $200 a night. We decided we were going to take a scenic train to Houston, Texas. The Amtrak train went through New Orleans, Louisiana and all the other bayou states, including Mississippi.

It was fun trying to smoke weed on a train in the luggage compartment with the top half of the door open to let fresh air in. We arrived in Houston around 11pm the next night, almost broke. I don't know how but we managed to spend nearly all of the money that we had robbed. I called a cab and when we jumped in, I asked the driver where the good clubs were in town. He gave us a ride to a motel in close proximity to potential bars to work.

I was exhausted, so I rested up the entire next day, and paid for one more night's stay. We were completely broke by this time. My boyfriend was waiting for money to be wired from his dad at 6pm that evening. The motel manager asked us to leave because we hadn't paid for the room that day and he wouldn't wait any longer.

We packed a few belongings, along with the extra spare blanket from the top shelf of the closet in the room. Somehow, I knew that we would need it, even though we had sleeping bags. I called for a cab, knowing full well that we didn't have the money to pay the driver to take us anywhere. But I knew that faith could move mountains. The driver showed up and I went out to his car alone, getting into the backseat.

I told him, "Look, I need you to help me out here. I'm new to town and I don't have any money to pay you right now but I need to get off this property with my boyfriend. If you will give us a ride out to a patch of woods I saw just outside of town as we were coming here the other night as soon as I get into a club, I swear and I promise I will pay you back." The driver agreed to oblige. He took us where I asked to go.

The distance outside of town must have been at least a few miles. I didn't realize it was that far. There we were, dropped off in the dark of night making our way into the woods. Just as we found a spot to settle, the thunder crashed and it began to downpour. We huddled together under the stolen blanket.with our belongings. We managed to not get wet and neither did our stuff which was pretty amazing.

The next morning, it was bright and sunny. We smoked some hand-rolled cigarettes, while I put my make-up on and got my sexy "Midnight" vibe going. I then made sure my dance bag was together to be sure I didn't forget anything, as we had to walk the miles back to town. After camouflaging our belongings with brush and leaves, we walked into town on the edge of a waterway canal. I was hired right away at a club and I made $400 by the end of the night.

We could have easily stayed in a motel room, but the few miles that we had to walk back out to the woods was kind of romantic. The entire rendezvous was very clandestine. We eventually bought a car then drove back up to Pennsylvania, due to his father becoming ill. As with all of my past relationships, ours ended after a few months so I went back out on the road to make my way to South Dakota. I had been back in South Dakota for a few months.

One Friday night, I went to a bar with one of my biker friends. We were in the town of Hill City which is a hop, skip and jump if you followed the 1880s train railroad route from Keystone. When we walked into The Mangy Moose, we were both drawn to a young couple and started up a conversation with them. Strange as it was, the woman left and headed to the restroom or somewhere, while at the same time, my friend walked over to the pool table to get a game going.

The remaining guy and I were left just sitting there. As we began to talk, we were both blown away within minutes. Turns out he was not only from York, Pennsylvania- it was his mother to whom I had spoken to years earlier at the Children's Home of York. His mother handled my case. She retired shortly after our phone call when I got the non-identifying information about myself from her.

How bizarre! What a small world! I am a firm believer in everything happening for a reason but this was almost too much! How could the stars line up at that precise moment? What is it that happens out there in the cosmos to make a strange occurrence like this happen? Blown away is still the only description I can conjure for that moment in time. Or Serendipity.

I was hooking up with all the wrong types of men, for different reasons I suppose. I believe one major reason was, as it has been noted, a girl chooses men that resemble her father. If that is true, then a lot of my experiences could be explained. It seemed like that is exactly what I got. Dysfunctional, mentally and physically abusive men, who little by little eroded what little bit of self- worth and esteem I had left within myself.

The second reason I believe was that my heart, soul and subconscious had remained shattered from losing my childhood and losing my children. The loss of my children and not being able to be a part of their lives was a pain that I didn't think would ever go away.

Because of the prevalent and enduring pain and suffering of depression,

I chose men with whom I thought I could change with nurturing and love into a good man who wouldn't hurt me in any way. In many of my relationships, I was playing Russian Roulette with my life and well-being.

ROAD TO NOWHERE

In the summer of 1999, I had already been working awhile at the Red Garter Saloon in Keystone. The Ruby House Restaurant was next-door with a divider in between. Both were filled with pristine, priceless treasures and antiques, along with an antique gun collection that was deemed the largest in the west. I had to dress, along with the other cocktail waitresses, as an old-time saloon girl. The uniform was cute with a red and black ruffled skirt that was hiked up on the side with a black, fringy shirt that slid off the shoulders.

As I would walk into town each morning from my house, children would say things like, "Mommy, look at the pretty lady!" I did feel like a saloon girl, right out of the 1880s, and it showed that I loved to play the part. I kept to myself, not really making too many friends except for Jerry Allen who lived next door to me and was the nighttime music entertainment at the saloon. Big Dave Murra was also my friend and we would all party at my house at night after work. The two guys performed the Wild West show during the day and I was the announcer on the microphone depicting the unfolding events to the tourists who all stopped to watch the show.

I was walking down the boardwalk after work as I made my way home, when I saw a Native American man walking towards me. He looked young, but he still intrigued me. He introduced himself as Will and his cousin who was with him, as Cody. After partying together a few times, I invited them to stay at my house. They had been staying in the dorms that were owned by their employer.

Also, my motives were not entirely for them, I wanted Will. Before long, he was my boyfriend and in my bed he landed. I was 28 and he was 19. My little bungalow house was full every night when we partied with coworkers after work. Will didn't like to be away from his home on Pine Ridge Reservation so he left and went back down.

Before he and Cody left, he asked if his other cousin Colton could stay at my house to work. He had just come up from Pine Ridge and needed a place to stay. I said I didn't mind. It was nice to have company. I was working 12 hour shifts, so I decided I would make him massage my feet at night in exchange for rent. He didn't mind pampering me and my feet were always killing me.

Just before I met Colton, I began talking to Justin and Jeremy a few times a week. I was also in the process of trying to get their father to let them come up and stay with me over their summer vacation. It was July, the busiest time of the tourist season when Rich agreed to allow the children to come stay with me. The problem was, at the same time I was told I needed to have my appendix removed. It explained the pain I was experiencing in my right side as I was trying to be a good cocktail waitress. I had the surgery and two days later, I hired my friend to let me drive his vehicle down to pick up my sons in Florida.

I was so happy they were back in my life, as they were now 8 and 9 years old. We left Keystone at 8 am on a Sunday morning and I drove most of the way, with the hammer down. We arrived in Tampa on Monday night, around 5 pm. Having painkillers the entire way helped my driving endurance and enjoyment of the drive . As we were getting closer, Justin and Jeremy kept calling my cell phone, wondering how much longer it would be before I came to pick them up.

I ended up having to call Mabel to borrow $200 to make the trip back to Keystone. She was actually nice and gave it to me with no meanness or contempt. When we finally got on our way, it was nearly 11pm that night. We decided to stop in Clearwater to play on the beach for a while. Everything was lit up, including the volleyball courts and playground. The children and I walked out over the pier where people were fishing. I was so happy to have them running ahead of me, even though I was in extreme pain.

Jeremy couldn't seem to stop saying the words Mom, Mommy and Mama, which I loved. Like typical children, each of them were showing off for me, doing what they were good at. I was so proud to be their mother and for the first time since the war began, I was allowed to fulfill that role. As we pulled out of Tampa on 75 North, I kept looking in the back at my children that had grown so much since I had last seen them last. They looked so content lying on the comfortable bed I had made for them.

Jeremy looked up at me and asked if I would hold him and sing him to sleep like I used to. I had always sung Hush Little Baby to them as babies- he remembered. My little house in Keystone was nothing more than a summer retreat, formerly a dorm to house workers. Because we all worked in the restaurant, there was no official kitchen in the home.

I tried to spend as much time as I could with the children while at the same time trying to recover from the appendectomy and continuing to work 10 hour days. The kids were on the phone a few times a day, talking with their dad from home sickness. The boys liked hanging out with the older guys and listening to their stories about life as a Native American and what it was like to live on a Reservation. My native friends would take them fishing, hiking and out into the woods where they would look for willow branches and also down to the recreational center while I was working. I was thankful for their help.

The children would still be asleep when I left for work in the mornings. I was still in a great deal of pain from the appendectomy surgery, but each day I was healing as I forced myself to walk and work. I was making really good money but there was never enough time to do anything fun with the children at night. All of the tourist attractions were closed for the day by the time I got off of work. I could sense that something bad was going to happen but I had no idea of what and when.

It was nearly 3 weeks into their visit when they started acting very belligerent and began to express their anger towards me for not being in their lives over the past years. I did the best I could under the circumstances to try to be the better parent and not bash their father in any way. I told them the absolute truth. I didn't know that throughout the day when they were on the phone with Rich, he was manipulating and brain-washing them while filling their heads with even more poison towards me.

I could tell that something was going on because when I returned home that night they were distant and standoffish but wanted to go across the street to the store to buy unnecessary things like more candy and soda. I had already given them close to $30 each throughout the course of the day. Just as I was coming through the door, they were both demanding I give them more money to go across the street to buy their chips and pop. I knew how much junk they had already consumed that day so I told them no. They started to throw a fit.

They were yelling and calling me derogatory names. Justin ran out the door and down the street and Jeremy was going to do the same but I reached out and grabbed him by his wrist and said, "It is almost midnight, you are not going out at this hour!" He let out a squeal as if I had hurt him which I didn't, then threw himself down on the floor in what can only be likened to as a temper-tantrum. Will and Cody had come up for a visit from the Rez and along with Colton, were sitting around observing the scene. Will offered to go after Justin, who was over on the payphone across the street talking to Rich.

At the same moment Will walked out the door, Jeremy sprang up and ran out to Justin at the payphone, to talk with his dad too. I wasn't even out of my work clothes yet but I ran barefoot across the street and tried to regain some control of the situation. My first attempt was to tell the children to go back to the house with Will, so I could talk to Rich.

He began accusing me of abusing Jeremy, when in truth, I only grabbed his wrist and as always, the conversation diminished with him yelling, not talking, as I was trying to do. After I finally hung up on him, I thought perhaps I could sit (which I desperately needed to do) and talk about what was really going on with the children. I changed my clothes and took a quick shower. When I got out, the house was empty.

Just then, everyone came in through the back door. There was still tension; hatred, resentment and anger filled the air. I tried to dispel it by offering to watch a video and making popcorn. The children could not be consoled and it was clear they hated me. Within the hour, a Pennington County Sheriff's deputy was knocking on my front door.

At first, I thought the police were there because the neighbor called about the disturbance or something. It turned out that one of my children had called. They made a complaint that I was abusing them at the urging of their father. I was dumb-founded. I couldn't believe my children would make up such a vicious lie.

I had continued to smoke marijuana in my life so during a thorough search of the house, a deputy found my stash in a little container with rolling papers and a bowl to go with it. It was not much pot but enough for the deputy to threaten me with a possession and paraphernalia charge. It was my guess at that point, the boys lied and told their dad that I was being abusive during their entire stay with me or something to that effect. As the deputy was searching my bedroom, he found Colton laying down beside my bed, attempting to hide.

I had no idea he was still there. It was nice to know that I had not been completely abandoned in one of my darkest hours. When he was questioned as to why he was hiding, he told the police that he had nowhere else to go. Jeremy and Justin were especially fond of Colton so they made sure the deputy knew he was their friend and they were mad at me, not him.

The succession of events felt like a whirlwind nightmare. Before I knew it, the children were being taken out of my home by Child Protection Services and being flown back to Florida. No charges were brought against me.Colton and I were standing in the middle of the knotty pine paneled living room looking at each other. He took me into his arms as I thought, "Why? Why did this happen?" I cried so hard.

My knees almost gave out on me so we sat there in the middle of the floor and he continued to hold me while I continued to cry. I had some leftover beers from their party earlier, and with the house being completely empty, we sat in the back room getting drunk by candlelight. We listened to a homemade cassette tape that someone had made of their favorite songs. We went to bed and made love with drunken passion.

All the anger and hostility I felt from the earlier events had dissipated with a newfound feeling. Laying down with Colton made me feel like no other man had ever made me feel and not just in a sexual way. At the time he was 21. We continued growing closer as time went on and we fell in love. It felt like he was my soulmate in the deepest sense of the word. Little did I know. We are destined to learn valuable lessons from soulmates not necessarily be bound together for life. Will and Cody headed back to the Pine Ridge Reservation.

Up until the time Colton and I got together, I had only heard stories of life on the Rez. As with any other destination in life, until you spend some time there you cannot understand the way of living and what everyday existence entails.

FAR BEHIND

Shannon County and Pine Ridge Reservation are one of the poorest areas in the United States. The unemployment rate on the Reservation is extremely high- somewhere around 98%. It is not so much the fact that people don't want to work, there are simply not enough jobs or resources for employment to go around. Lack of housing is also a major issue. Some households have many family members living under the same roof. The average household consists of two, three and four families.

Not everyone receives commodities or checks from the government each month. The commodities do offer a large brick of cheese which is sometimes called yellow gold because it is so tasty you can sell it for cash. Powdered milk, powdered eggs, canned meat and potatoes also came with commodities. Food stamps and grant checks or welfare would cover most other expenses.

Once a year, the carnival comes to the town of Pine Ridge, as well as the largest Lakota Sioux Nation Pow Wow. Fancy dancers and ladies in their jingle dresses with the drumbeat pounding into your soul, is a beautiful sight. The Rez has its own radio station, KILI which plays a variety of music including Lakota singers and daily discussions about subjects that affect the people. Usually, from the first of the month to the 15th, those who like to party do so until the money runs out. There are many people however who consider themselves sacred and they do their part in continuing the traditional ways, language and beliefs of the Lakota people.

Despite the living conditions at Colton's cousin Kent's home, I found myself with a sense of family and comfort that I craved. In the winter, while sitting around a wood-burning stove, the camaraderie immensely outweighed any discomfort from lack of amenities. After we moved into our own trailer, I didn't like Kent for a long time. I could not understand why every single time, when Colton would leave me to go on a drinking binge, he would always wind up eventually at Kent's never-ending party. The two of them grew up together and were very close.

No matter how many times I begged Kent to turn Colton away and steer him home to me, he never would. I guess one good thing came of it when I did try to find Colton, I always knew where to look first. Even though I was labeled as a white woman who was stuck up and no fun along with other more derogatory names by Kent, his mother always welcomed me in. She would point to the back room where Colton would be lying, passed out. Though usually drunk himself, Kent never disrespected me because he knew the love Colton and I had for each other and he knew our hearts were true to one another.

For the longest time it was unfathomable to me as to why people would live in such destitute circumstances, but was never my place to question but I did seek the answers. Colton would occasionally tell me stories of his childhood. One was a favorite game the kids called played hooky. They would grab onto the back bumper of a car and let it pull them all around on the snow packed roads which hardly ever saw a plow. There are a lot of wild dogs running around and it causes people to walk around with big sticks to ward off an attack if necessary.

The local favorite pastime is cruising around, hanging out with friends and visiting. In the town of Pine Ridge, there were two stores that sold gasoline: Big Bats Texaco and the other was called Yellow Bird's, where I worked for a few months. I am pretty sure I got the job because the owner was white. Big Bats was geared towards tourists passing through and a great place to eat good food, buy pop or whatever else you might need for your travels. Yellow Bird's catered to the children and locals by offering inexpensive toys, candy, popcorn and ice cream.

There are a few people who earn a living by selling popovers, a meat filled pastry, along with Indian Tacos. Fry bread is used to make an Indian Taco. These delicious culinary creations are served right out of a van or car. There is no need to question the preparation process; they are so good you don't care. Around the first of every month, in the parking lot of the Sioux Nation shopping center, a flea market was set up that offered all kinds of items.

Vendors sold jackets and T-shirts that said, "Native Pride," along with other sayings. I particularly loved the beadwork by natives at the market, so whenever I could find a beautiful necklace or earrings I bought them without concern of the price.

I learned the hard way about alcohol abuse. If I brought alcohol home, the events following would inevitably lead to disaster. Colton is a violent drunk. It didn't matter what kind of alcohol, he could never consume it with responsibility. If I had a bottle of dinner wine, and he couldn't find the corkscrew, he would use a knife or whatever he could find to break up the cork until he got to the wine. If I bought a case of beer and foolishly assumed it would last a week or month, it would be gone the very same night.

I did not want him to drink at all because every time he did, I ended up getting hurt. I could never prevent alcoholism from coming into the home, but I did prevent him from stealing my money and spending it at a bar. There was nothing to keep Colton and I tied down and he was ready to travel and see the country outside of South Dakota.

We bought an old 1979 station wagon, otherwise known on the Rez as a grocery getter. We bought it from a shop owner in town. He knew everything I had just gone through and he knew me well enough to know that it was definitely time for me to move on. I didn't care how ugly the car looked. I just wanted to get out onto the wild open road again with my new love to start our new life.

I danced a few nights in Rapid City at Shotgun Willies to get some travel money for us to get to Denver. I took off work one night so we decided to go to The Oasis in Rapid, a predominantly Native bar downtown. I thought we were having a good time but as it turned out, Colton was seething with jealousy because I had been talking to a man earlier at the bar.

After we left, I had just turned onto a back road, when Colton smashed his fist onto the dashboard, causing it to crack in several places. He then punched the windshield, nearly putting his hand through it. The impact created a spiderweb in the glass. I pulled over and parked because it felt like he might hit me next and I didn't want to wreck the car. He continued to rant, saying that I had invited the white man's advances in order to make him jealous.

No matter how much I tried to reason with him, he remained in a rage because he was so overly intoxicated. I feared saying too much because I was not sure if he was capable of seriously hurting me. He then switched his rage towards me and pushed me a few times up against the window which caused my head to hit the glass and I screamed out. I must have scared him into reality because he jumped out while yelling at himself as to how he could allow his anger to be targeted at me that way. He calmed down enough to get back into the car so I started driving again, heading out towards the woods to park for a while.

Before we reached our favorite spot, Colton was passed out. I sat there in the pitch black darkness, on the warm hood of the car asking myself what business I had trying to be with a Native American man. Maybe I was crossing some line looking for trouble? No, I knew that he loved me, he was just drunk. The next morning when he woke up, he did not remember any of the events which had transpired the night before.

In my mind I thought if he could not remember, maybe it wouldn't happen again. We continued on with our plans to leave South Dakota. He attributed all of this pent-up anger and desire to drink from being so close to where he grew up on the Reservation. It made sense to me.

HELLRAISER

We decided to head out that day for Denver. We traveled the route to Colorado that went through Wyoming, which revealed a very important detail we had overlooked. We didn't own the car for very long so we didn't notice that the gas tank gauge always read half full, no matter how much fuel was in the tank. The needle was stuck! So there we were, out in the middle of nowhere. I felt like prey in no man's land, waiting for the buzzards to start hovering in circles above us. So what happens? We ran out of gas of course.

Colton and I walked a little bit before we saw there was a ranch up ahead. He continued to walk the rest of the way, and I stayed behind sitting with my Doberman Pagan, in the car. The rancher was nice enough to drive his truck to the car and brought a gas can so we could get to where his gas supply was on his ranch. He filled our gas tank full to the brim without charging us a cent. We were on our way again and pulled into Colorado around 10 pm that night and pulled into Denver a little after midnight.

We then found a motel room that accepted pets. We fell asleep with thoughts of the following day running through our minds. We would both be looking for work and we agreed that I would find a club to dance in first, then he would find a regular job to accommodate my hours during the day. In Denver, there is a really great vibe. I was hired at a small, out of the way mom-and-pop place called The Paper Tiger which had a loyal blue collar clientele. I chose a small, less than desirable bar to work, until I got more familiar with the main clubs I was after in town.

It was a comfortable place to get started. To save money, Colton and I started to go to the truckstop to shower and eat after my shift. We would then head up to the mountains to find a place to park and sleep. During the day we spent all of our time in nature, exploring and discovering new and beautiful places.
We didn't need a ton of money, we were rich in love and just being together. Many times, even though it was very cold in some places up in

the mountains, I would wash my hair and bathe in a stream to get ready for work. It was such a wonderful feeling to be out in nature after spending all night in a smoke-filled bar.

I was making good money. I told Colton he didn't have to work or he could take his time finding a job. On the nights I worked, he would park in the back parking area, with the permission of the owners. He was fine, safely sitting out in the lot waiting for me to get off work. He didn't have a pair of much needed glasses and he couldn't see to drive at night anyway. Driving in a big city made him feel very uneasy and downright scared so he would read or keep himself occupied some other way.

I asked him to come in a few times while I was on my shift. He said he couldn't rationalize spending $3.50 for a beer. I think he was truly making an effort to stop drinking altogether. He assured me that he was fine, sitting out in the parking lot with Pagan, walking him whenever he needed it. Our brakes had worn down from driving up and into the mountains. One night at the bar, I performed a few dances for a guy who worked at Midas and he gave me a business card and told me to keep in touch.

A few days afterwards, Colton and I headed out to one of our favorite places, knowing full well that the brakes were on their way out. Like other important details, I put the issue onto the back burner in matters of importance. We wanted to concentrate on more important things, like being in love and being in the wild. We were on a dirt road that only had a slight incline. I was the one driving, when all of a sudden the brakes went completely out.

Even at a small incline, with no brakes to slow down, you pick up speed at an amazing rate. Before I knew it, we were going close to 30 mph and going faster as I whipped us around those curves. I was terrified! We were missing large boulders to the left and right by inches. After I was able to come to a complete stop, we flagged down a park ranger who then gave us a ride into the small town that we were near. I called the guy from the Midas shop and explained my situation.

He came out and fixed the brakes temporarily and then guided us back into Denver to the shop where he fixed the brakes, completely free of charge. He even paid for a room for the night. It was times like these, the awesome perks helped me know why I loved being a stripper and exotic dancing so much. It seemed as though within the few moments of a dance I could entrance a man to the point of him almost being bewitched and would do almost anything for me.

No matter where we were driving, I was always paranoid that a cop would pull us over and run my name, discovering that I had warrants so we were always extra cautious. We registered the car in Colton's name. We did end up having a few interactions with the police, all of which were for the cracked windshield. Each time, they only asked for Colton's license and insurance card and that was usually enough to send them on their way, with a warning to get the windshield fixed.

I had one particularly good night at the bar. It wasn't so much good in terms of money, as it was in dealing with decent people who appreciated me. After work, I went out to the car and Colton was stretched out in the back, sleeping. I told him to stay comfortable and I would get us out to the truck stop. As we got onto the highway, we were talking as he was waking up. He reached his arm up around my neck from behind and kissed me, pulling me close to him as I was driving.

As we were traveling down the highway, there was a rust colored truck, which for a minute or two was right beside us in the passing lane. He was beginning to freak me out so Colton told me to slow down in order for him to pass us but that didn't work so I sped up. The driver exited onto the ramp after a few miles. Colton still had his arm around me. As we were nearing the truckstop exit, we noticed a helicopter with the spotlight on right above us, appearing to be almost aimed at our car.

Colton and I commented on it but then dismissed it, thinking they were looking for someone and we just happened to be in their path. As soon as we pulled into the truckstop, Colton jumped out because he had to use the restroom, while I made my way to a parking spot. Within minutes of our arrival, six police cars surrounded me in the parking lot. I had just put Pagan on his leash to let him out. I looked at them while wondering what Colton could have possibly done while I had been at work.

As Colton was coming out, the police were questioning me about whom I was traveling with. I told them Colton was my boyfriend. They put him up against the car and patted him down. We were both in confusion asking the police what was going on. They told us, as it turned out, the strange man on the highway in the truck had called the police because Colton had his arm up around my neck. The passerby assumed it was a potential hostage situation or something crazy like that. They had nothing to go on so instead of a wasted trip, they decided to search the car which took another hour. They found nothing.

GONE AWAY

We continued to head east out of Colorado. There was nothing we confirmed and no one was going to keep us there. We were headed back to Pennsylvania because I was eager to show Colton where I grew up. I couldn't wait to return to my old stomping grounds. We went right to the area where I lived last at the base of the Pocono Mountains, in the town of Lehighton. After crossing the country, when we got there we were nearly out of cash.

We found a nice little patch of woods beside a cornfield which was well concealed with tall corn because the season was well into autumn, just before harvest season. I found a club right away to dance and the situation was pretty much the same as when we left Denver- while I worked, Colton would wait for me outside in the car.

It was also a small mom-and-pop place called Sandy's. The owners would offer Colton odd jobs from time to time. Even though there was not a lot of business, I made enough for us to live comfortably. Meanwhile, we were able to save for an apartment.
We were back for about three weeks when a man I used to work for came into the club. I had only worked with Dennis for two days. I hadn't seen him in over a year since I last left Pennsylvania.

The year before I had been searching for a regular job and I came across an ad for a laborer with a local home construction framing company. I wasn't sure what the job entailed but I liked the pay of $8.00 an hour as a starting wage. I called and asked the owner of the company Dennis, if he thought a girl could do the job. He and I talked for a while, when I discreetly told him that I was really a stripper/exotic dancer and I only needed a job for a week or two for extra money.

Of course being a man, his interest was heightened instantly with me. I had enough money to get into a hotel room for two nights. I called Dennis back and told him I would call him on the following night to tell him exactly where I was. I called Dennis, who lived only a few exits away. After asking if I was hungry, he said he would come get me so we could get some dinner and talk about the job. When he arrived, we walked next door to a restaurant and ordered some food to go, then headed back to the room.

He explained what would be involved, being a laborer and also told me that framing was hard work. I was sure I still wanted the job and I assured him I thought I could handle it. He told me he would pick me up the next morning at 6am and also advised me to dress warm. When I awoke, the fresh and crisp morning air along with a cup of coffee made the heightened anticipation of the day a little more exciting. Dennis told me that he was going to pick me up, then we would go pick up his crew at a designated meeting place, then be on our way to the job site. At first, the guys were shocked to see a female and wondered exactly what benefit there was in having me there, except for the obvious reason to watch a curvy chick working beside them all day.

The morning was cold enough that there was frost on everything at the worksite. Gloves made it slightly easier for me to carry sheets of tongue and groove plywood. Midway through the day, my body was beginning to seriously ache. Near the end of the afternoon, the guys were up on the second floor and asked me to hand them up a piece of plywood. I couldn't do it. That was it, my ass was kicked and I was done for.

I struggled through the next day and in the evening accepted that the job was too physically demanding. I called someone for a ride, checked out of the motel room and set out into the world again. Dennis didn't know where he could find me or send my paycheck.

Back to the present. It was just after noon at the bar. I was up on stage when I saw Dennis walk through the door. He seemed to look as though he was mystified and couldn't believe it was really me. When I stepped off the stage and stood there talking to him, he proceeded to tell me how he searched for me on the days following my disappearance so he could pay me the wages he owed me. He then went out to his truck for his checkbook.

It was a particularly slow day, so extra cash was welcome. He came back in with a check for $150.00, not bad for a day and a half of work.

Right then, the dollar signs like miniature cash registers in my mind rang and popped up for another potential Sugar Daddy #4.

WHAT YOU GIVE

It is hard to explain, but when you possess a man with female charm, they have no choice but to do as you say with pleasure in doing it. I began the game as always, portraying the poor little defenseless woman with no place to stay, no car and just struggling to survive. I never mentioned my lover, Colton. A few nights after seeing Dennis that day in the bar and enjoying a few dinners together, he paid for a week's rent at the same motel I had met him at previously. He then told me to look for an apartment. After I found one, he gave me $1800.00 cash to move in.

Then in increments of a few hundred dollars at a time, he gave me money to furnish the apartment and pay the bills. I filled our new home with antiques and vintage furniture. Dennis would take me shopping and while we were browsing, I could make his mind go crazy by merely mentioning that under my long dress, I wasn't wearing panties. Comments like that could make him spend thousands in one swoop. All the while, I was making him believe that he was my boyfriend.

I convinced him not long after to give me $5000.00. In truth, there was no reason, except for the fact that I wanted to see that amount of money and I wanted to feel how I felt holding it. I told him that I needed it for a computer which I really did buy but after, I ended up returning it so I could keep the cash. He bought something for me with his Visa card and by using the receipt, account numbers and expiration date, I made multiple mail order purchases, which were mostly for Justin and Jeremy. I thought it would be devilishly funny to buy them an electric guitar and set of drums! Rich didn't think it was funny.

Dennis definitely didn't think it was funny when he received the bill and then he was even less humorous with me when he came over that night. While peering through the windows, he saw Colton. Livid is the only word that comes to mind. When I knew Dennis had discovered him, after letting him in I just played it off and told him that he was only my travel partner.

I told him that he was from the Pine Ridge Reservation and I was showing him the sights of the east coast. That was the beginning of a very twisted triangle. Dennis and Colton were well aware of each other but I was able to convince Dennis that Colton was only my friend. I was madly in love with Colton and that would be the reason why I was blind to ever increasing violence. I thought the violence was magnified because he was out of his element in a new world. I could understand that my obsession with playing men is not wise when you are with a man who is already insecure.

In some ways I felt the games could make any man violent. Life with a dancer was new to Colton and all the worldly vices I craved for years were new to him as well. Justin and Jeremy were on their Christmas vacation and they wanted to come up to visit us. From Pennsylvania to Florida on Interstate 95, I could get to Tampa in a little over 18 hours. Colton came along and the trip went smooth all the way down and back.

One night when Dennis came over, Colton and the boys were in the kitchen, in the back of the apartment. I thought Colton would tell them things like the truth of what role Dennis played in all of our lives and in my life especially. Instead, he was calling me a whore to my children and getting them to disrespect me all over again, just like Rich did. Ultimate betrayal and treachery. Yes, I was playing Dennis, but no I was not sleeping with him.

Everyone sure enjoyed all the money coming into the household that got spent fast, with no regard of what I had to deal with in order to get it. It didn't matter about the amount of intelligence it took to get that kind of money from someone- without giving up my body. At that time, Dennis had given me a little over $30,000. The rest of the boys' visit was strained. It was near the time for me to return them to Florida and I had tolerated just about enough of Coltons abuse, so I threw him out.

That started a war with Justin and Jeremy. They called Rich, who in turn called the police again with glee for no reason. I hadn't done anything wrong so I wasn't that shaken when the State Troopers arrived. It did hurt bad that my children were idolizing abusers. They were mad at me for kicking Colton out. I didn't want to make him leave, I just didn't know what else to do. After the officers did they're investigating, I agreed to allow Colton to come back home for the sake of the children.

The day arrived for them to return to Florida so Pagan, the children and I headed back down to Tampa, while Colton stayed to watch over the house. I needed to be away from him for a while.

After I returned from Tampa, the arguing and discord continued. Dennis was threatening to not give me any more money if I continued to allow Colton to stay at the house. Being tired of it all anyway, Dennis and I drove Colton to the bus station in downtown Allentown. Dennis purchased a one way ticket for him back to South Dakota. I acted tough, like I was glad to see him go but it broke my heart to put him on that bus.

I knew deep down that he and I needed a break. He had to realize how much we needed each other in the life we shared. An hour or two after Dennis and I dropped Colton off, it felt as though my heart weighed 100 pounds. I missed Colton so much. I blamed myself for needing to have mad money and luxury items that neither Colton nor I could afford. He wasn't back in Pine Ridge for more than a day before I began calling and telling him how my entire body ached for him.

It was only two days later that I sent him a ticket out of Rapid City, to come back to me. His bus went through Pittsburgh so I decided I needed a tiny road trip for myself. I left and drove a few hours to meet him. The bus pulled into the station at nearly 3am. I loved this man and I couldn't wait to be near him again, no matter how much he hurt me. It hurt worse not having him in my life.

Dennis became suspicious of Colton having returned when I would refuse to open the door for him. He would stand outside on the front porch pounding on the door, and then would go around to each and every window. Pagan, being the watchdog he was bred to be, was also the main protector of the house. It was always a big commotion which would wear on anyone's nerves.

We decided to sell the contents of the house in order to get on the road. I couldn't let Dennis know that Colton and I were indeed a couple and we were back together. My gravy train would have ended for sure.

ROCKSTAR

I decided it would be easier to get money and manipulate him from afar. We left Pennsylvania and went south on Interstate 81 to make our way to Nashville Tennessee. I loved the town, as I had returned several times since being a runaway to dance and I knew there would always be an abundance of work. We made it to Indiana before the car broke down on the side of the road. We were close enough to an exit ramp that we were able to coast all the way into a Walmart parking lot. It was very cold and the dogs were huddled beneath a few blankets and sleeping bags.

Along with Pagan, we now had a new female Doberman pup I named Serena. I had to wait for two hours before I could call Dennis to ask him for assistance. It always helped to make him feel like I needed him to tell me what I should do, when in fact I knew full well what needed to be done. By the time I was finally able to reach him, I spent another hour convincing him to wire me $1,000 for repairs. When I got back out to the car, Colton was really pissed off because he was freezing and was also bitter about me having the comfort of standing in a nice warm entryway on the payphone.

I called a tow truck, which took us to a shop, then gave us a ride to a Super 8. The garage had an account with the hotel, so we didn't have to spend an arm and a leg for a room, not that I really cared. It wasn't my money. Before getting out, I asked the tow truck driver if he knew of any exotic dance bars around town. He told me where the good ones were with a bemused smile on his face. It was at this time I became quite proficient in spinning lies to Dennis, as well as getting everyone else around me to lie whether it was the mechanic at the shop or the desk clerk at a hotel.

If I promised to take care of them with a big tip, I could get people to say or do pretty much anything I wanted with regards to a Sugar Daddy. Money does buy happiness. The car was fixed and Colton and I were on our way. When we arrived in Nashville, we checked into a motel which was located in a rather shady part of town. It was hard to find a room that would accommodate our dogs. I didn't care, as long as I had everything that was important to me close by. I was hired by Déjà Vu and worked for a few nights before I started to feel sad and depressed.

When we first began the road trip, Colton and I were having an extensively deep conversation. I made the mistake of going into detail of what I had to do in order to survive as a teenager, then later do escort and dates by choice. Ever since that conversation, whenever we got into an argument, which was becoming more and more frequent, Colton could never resist the opportunity to call me a whore. Of course, he knew that it was the lowest of blows because it was obvious how much shame I still carried with me over it.

After a while, I didn't even want to dance anymore with him, making me feel so dirty, ugly and cheap. Deep down, I wanted to be pure again. Untarnished and treated like the good woman I knew I was. I was so busy blaming myself, I was still blind to Colton's ever worsening violence and anger towards me. With the abuse from previous boyfriends and now Colton, I blamed myself for pushing them over the proverbial edge. I could always find an excuse for them as they were mistreating me; it was definitely not a good time however for me to come to this revelation.

Every man I had ever been with was dependent on my income. Colton always said he wanted to work, yet he would never make the effort to grab the reins so I could have other options. Then, to make matters worse, he said he didn't want us to rely on Dennis anymore. I understood his request but the need to wander kept me hooked and I was not going to give up the support from Dennis.

I had to depend on him or we would have been homeless and on the streets. Instead, because of him and his money, we had a roof over our heads and food in our bellies, and a car that ran every single day. I would spend hours on the phone with Dennis while Colton was sitting only a few feet away from me, listening to me spin the lies like a black widow luring my prey to my newest web. It wasn't terribly hard because Dennis was overly eager to be tangled. The hard part was Colton needed to be completely silent and at times, going into a silent rage because of the things I would say.

Anyone listening to my conversations with Dennis would have been completely convinced that what I was saying was the truth but to me it was a game that required mastery. To be able to achieve this feat, I had to make myself believe the lies right along with them. Colton and I were leaving Nashville when the car really broke down. I knew it would happen, but again we managed to get the car off the highway and into a gas station parking lot.

I had about $600.00 wired and called for a tow truck. We were in the town of Murfreesboro, still close to Nashville. There wasn't a local tow company which would go back to Nashville, so we had to wait a few hours for one to come from Nashville. I went back to work for a few nights at Déjà Vu, using taxis to transport me but that was not good enough. We needed wheels.

So began another plot for even more money from Dennis. I asked for a $2000.00 wire, which I intended to buy a used car and promised to get back on Interstate 81 north, to head back to him in Pennsylvania. I didn't buy a car. Instead, we just lived it up by going shopping and not having a care in the world. When the money was almost gone, I started panicking again. This time when I called Dennis, I told him that I wanted to stay in Nashville for a little while longer because I was doing well.

I explained the money he had just sent went to expensive shoes and costumes that were a necessity in my trade. It could've been true. I then went on to convince him to take a few days off of work and come down to Tennessee to visit me. I didn't have to go into great detail because he had it in his mind that this was to be the magical, romantic moment he had long awaited, to have sex with me.

A few hours passed then he was packed, on the road and on his way. Colton and I had about $100 left so the only logical place for Colton to hang out for an extended period was the McDonald's next door but first he had to go to the homeless mission and get a bed downtown. We both agreed it was what needed to be done. Plus, he said it would be a good opportunity to be more in the heart of town. He would go to one of the day labor agencies to find a job for daily pay.

I knew the speedy way Dennis always drove, breaking the speed limit usually going around 80, it would not be long before arrived. I gave Colton my cell phone then he set out with a little bit of money and went downtown. I felt bad, but at the same time, I wanted this ordeal to be over with. I knew this was more or less moving the game up to a higher level.

After a few days of having Dennis with me, I figured that I would have him programmed to do whatever I wanted. I had to figure out just what I could actually do without being unfaithful to Colton. Or even worse, falling into the actual category of being a whore. When he arrived, I greeted him wearing one of his favorite dresses and pair shoes which he bought me. He had a fetish for open toed shoes and pretty feet, so I made sure he knew my outfit was meant for him.

My mind was wandering and I couldn't help but wonder where Colton was and what he was doing at the moment. I knew as soon as I had a moment alone, I would be able to call him but I had no idea when the opportunity would arise. Dennis pleaded with me a bit so I agreed to take a shower with him. I figured as long as he could revel in my nudity, he would be satisfied. For the most part, that was true. Being a man though, with a hard dick, it was hard for me to step out and leave him hanging but I did.

That night Dennis insisted that we sleep in the same bed. All I could think about was how repulsive his body felt next to mine. It was like I was so determined to not let him have any part of me, being that up close and personal was too much. I couldn't stop wishing that I didn't have to deal with all of this but I knew in order to have the sweet, I had to take the bitter too. The following evening, Dennis made a reservation to have an exquisite dinner at Ruth's Chris Steakhouse. In a way, I felt sorry for him;

147

after all, he was trying so hard to win my affections, yet I was seemingly frigid.

We went back to the room that night and slept in separate beds, which broke his heart. I kept telling him that I wanted to be his girlfriend, but I was not ready to be intimate with him. I wasn't entirely comfortable with affection even with the men I loved.

The next day he was ready to go home. I guess I was trying to speed up the visit so much that he gave up trying. I had to convince him before he left that if he truly loved me as much as he said he did, he couldn't just leave me stranded with no transportation.

He thought for sure that he would've been able to convince me to go back to Pennsylvania with him. With defeated and low spirits, begrudgingly we began the search for a suitable vehicle looking across the used car lots of Nashville. We found a lot that had a surplus of minivans, which is exactly what I wanted; to me, they were perfect for traveling. The car lot was not far from the Waffle House and Motel 6 where I had been a teenager. I couldn't help but think of all the miles I have traveled since then.

In a few hours, after the purchase of the van and a few hundred dollars in my pocket, I got rid of Dennis as fast as I could so I could call Colton. I wanted to get him back into my arms, where he belonged. He was still a bit angry and agitated, but then he came to realize all that I had accomplished. Despite the temporary discomfort he endured, it was all worth it.

Acquiring things felt like what I can only guess feels like when a hunter gets a trophy for what he was going for. In the same respect, the merchandise was like a trophy to me. I always felt proud after the kill.

WONDERFUL

Colton had been talking to his family back in Pine Ridge off and on, so he was still very homesick. We decided to at least get back to Rapid City so we could be closer. He and I both knew if we went to Pine Ridge he would not be able to resist the temptations of alcohol. I don't know why I believed him when he assured me being in Rapid City would be different, yet we still made our way back. He had family everywhere it seemed. He began sneaking off to spend time with a cousin who had no real sense of responsibility either.

We were staying in a motel room which was only $100 per week. Because of the dogs and budget, we had to settle for another rundown place. You had to watch where you walked, or you might step on glass or even worse, a syringe. It only added to the sadness I was dealing with from Colton's abuse which continued to get worse. One afternoon we got into a huge argument.

He began to push me around so I ran into the bathroom. I had my back up against the toilet bowl and my legs outstretched on the floor, with my feet pressed up against the door so he couldn't get to me.
He was in such a rage and rammed the door so hard and so many times, the toilet cracked and all the water came spilling out all over me. Of course, because there was nothing for me to brace myself against, he smashed through the door and beat me.

He always managed to do the worst damage in areas that were not easily visible. That didn't keep me from knowing the bruises were still there. Just like the bruises in my childhood, the memories were starting to emerge whether I wanted them to or not. We left Rapid City and headed south again on our way somewhere. We stopped at Columbia, Missouri. Over the years, I created ways to conjure up money usually stemming from shoplifting.

I would steal merchandise and then return it for cash or I would buy something with a gift certificate that could be pawned. I purchased brand new merchandise with stolen credit cards and the goods went right to the pawnshop. I only ever received about a quarter of what the actual value was but it didn't matter as long as I acquired the money I was after to get a little farther down the road. In really desperate times I would take toiletry items I had bought from Walmart and added water to whatever it was: shampoo, conditioner or lotion. They would accept practically anything as a return item and give back up to $20.00 cash. Sometimes I would just steal items to return.

We went into the mall in Columbia, Missouri and I decided to steal a few bras from Sears. The checkout girl realized there was a discrepancy between the amount of items I took into the dressing room and what I came out with. When I walked out to the main part of the mall where Colton was, two large security guards approached us and demanded to look in my bag. They found the stolen bras so they took me to the security office, called the police and I was taken to jail. Because I had a previous felony, they set bail high for $5000.00 cash.

I talked to Dennis by calling collect, several times a day. Eventually, a few days later, he agreed to hire an attorney for me and put up the cash for my bond, as long as I agreed to come back to Pennsylvania. I was released, so Colton and I made our way to Pennsylvania. As soon as we got there, I had to devise a master plan to hide Colton. I think I persuaded Dennis to wire more money along the way so I could hide Colton in a motel room.

I went to Dennis's house and thought I could make him happy, though I was still not willing to have sex with him. It seemed like sex was the only thing his mind could focus on. I think the more you withhold sex, it just drives men immensely insane. Especially if they have been waiting for it. I think he was mostly thinking about all he had invested in me and wanted some type of return. The amount of money now was reaching upwards at around $73,000.

One of the ploys I used to save myself from his advances was the intense, growing pain in my side. In all truth, the pain was beginning to affect my entire life and especially my having sex with Colton. It got to the point that I didn't want to even dance for him for fear of getting him too aroused. That really blew his mind because after that, I didn't even want him to see me naked. I managed to get $1000.00 from him which I used to go west again on Interstate 80, with Colton.

I liked traveling on that highway because it would take us all away into Nebraska. We stopped at the 76 truck stop and took a shower before continuing on. The truckstop showers were in little rooms where you could lounge, rest and regroup as well as refresh.
I dropped Colton off in Rapid City because I had a court appearance in Missouri and I was on my way when I called Dennis and asked for more money. I told him that Colton found me and had stolen the van and went back down to the Reservation. Dennis would have to come out and give me a ride down to Missouri for my court appearance.

The fact that he had $5,000.00 cash riding on it, made it easy for me to convince him to come. The entire ride to Columbia with Dennis was rather somber for the most part. I think he knew I was going to hit him up for yet another vehicle. He was correct. His first priority was to get me to my court hearing. I could tell Dennis resented me for having the hold on him that I did, but he just kept on playing the game. He was hoping we could check into a hotel so he could finally get what he wanted, but I didn't give in.

After the court hearing in Missouri, we traveled towards South Dakota, first stopping in Omaha. I kept asking him to let me keep his truck and then he could fly home. Instead, he ended up renting me a minivan from the Omaha airport. It was a brand new Pontiac Montana that had only been driven once, with less than 50 miles on it. I kept that van for 6 months. My entire trip had been filled with lots of shopping so I had lots of bags. When we parted ways in the parking lot I asked him for $600.00 for gas and expenses. He gave it to me with a grudge.

I drove up to Pine Ridge to pick up Colton. Setting out on the road again, we really didn't have any particular destination but we wanted to take in more of the country. We had already traveled on most of the highways in the east and Midwest. At that time, I think my gypsy spirit was wearing off on him. We were headed towards Nashville again, just about out of money, so we stopped in Little Rock, Arkansas.

I went into a Walmart and spent nearly two hours pretending to shop. I was getting up my nerve to carry out a personal organizer that was worth $30.00. I don't know how many times I shoplifted before, at different Walmarts across the country, without a problem. This time was destined to be different. I acted like I forgot my wallet and I walked towards the front door. As I was passing through the security checkpoint, the alarm went off.

In its mechanical and embarrassing way, it announced that I had activated the alarm/theft system. I kept walking into the parking lot, not seeing Colton so I began to panic. I walked faster then threw the organizer under someone's car. I figured if it wasn't in my possession, they couldn't do anything.
Colton was slowly coming down the row in the van to pick me up and at the exact moment as I jumped into the van, three little old ladies were slowly crossing in front of us.

I couldn't get out of there fast enough. We got back out onto the highway and were still almost broke. I was pretty shook up over the ordeal so it took me an hour or so to calm down. We were almost out of gas when we came to the town of Fort Smith, Arkansas. It wasn't a stopping point by choice. We pulled into a Pilot truckstop so we could sleep in the van that night. We would look for work the next day.

Colton once again said he would perform day labor to get us going. I was determined to cut ties from Dennis because I knew that most of Colton's anger was from me interacting constantly with Dennis. He did not want Dennis in our lives anymore and neither did I. I found a bar called Regina's

House of Dolls and I began working at night while Colton worked during the day. At first, we lived at the truck stop for a few nights. The club had an account for the dancers to stay at a Best Western Hotel for $25 a night.

It was very nice compared to the motels we were used to settling for. We ended up staying at the hotel for nearly three months. My beloved Doberman Pagan began to act aggressively towards me when Serina went into heat. I believe the reason was that several times in the past, he had gotten into the trash and ripped up my used maxi pads. It didn't register as to what that actually meant for an animal. He had a taste for my blood.

Serena was in full blown heat, and Pagan bit my face. Thank goodness it was only a superficial wound but I still had to take time off of work because I didn't want to wear makeup until it healed. We decided to go back to Nebraska in Rushville, which is a straight shot below Pine Ridge. I had the misconception of thinking that we could be anywhere near the Reservation and Colton could resist alcohol temptations. He also had an aunt who lived in Rushville. I was looking through the newspaper for a place to live when I saw an ad for a one bedroom house for $200 a month. I called the owner and asked him to come to where I was, so I could follow him to the house.

The landlord took me to the home and while we were inside, I told him that I didn't have access to any money at the moment. I promised I would go to welfare and other agencies to get the rent and deposit money. I went on to tell the owner that I was a nude exotic dancer and would be happy to entertain him a few times a week, if he would cooperate with me. Within the hour, I was standing naked in his workshop across town, dancing to songs on the radio. I kept thinking about these things I did for survival. Survival of the fittest. We moved in that night.

We had been living in Rushville for only a few days before Colton was in the bars. He did manage to get a job working for one of the prominent business owners in town. I was a waitress at a small cafe with a bowling alley in the same building. We moved into a different home because after a while the landlord began to creep me out and was becoming a little too possessive. Plus, I really did not want to dance for him anymore.

On Colton's very first pay day, instead of coming straight home, he went straight to the bar. When I found him he became so irate he ended up punching out the window of the entry door to the establishment. The police were called and picked him up though I don't know what they did with him.

It was still a semi-early Saturday night and as I walked home, I remembered there was a bar to dance at over in the next town of Hay Springs, Nebraska. That town was even smaller than Rushville, which was hard to believe. It was around 6:30pm when I called and spoke to the owner of the Silver Dollar Saloon. I told him that I really needed to work and I was an excellent dancer and entertainer.

An hour later, he came and picked me up, with his young son in the backseat. He explained to me that his bar was the whiskey, redneck, hoot and holler, cowboy type of place. He assured me that there was generally a good crowd and I should do well. I made much more than I expected for such a small bar. I was very surprised that I had made over $400.00 in two hours. At the end of the night, the owner wanted to introduce me to a man named Lawrence, who had been sitting at the end of the bar all night.

The owner then told me that Lawrence was a driver for dancers and he would be giving me a ride home. He assured me Lawrence was very trustworthy and had been a family friend for years. When Lawrence dropped me off, he gave me his home phone number and told me that if I needed anything I could call him. Later that night, after Colton had not returned most likely in jail, I called Lawrence and asked if we could possibly go to breakfast the following morning. He agreed to pick me up at 7:00 am bright and early the next morning.

As we sat in the restaurant near Gordon, Nebraska, I explained to him what was going on in my life and asked if he could let me borrow one of his vehicles. By 11 o'clock that same morning, he had bought me a $1700.00 Chevy Cavalier! I really amazed myself sometimes. On his future visits, I would dance for him privately and he gave me nearly $1000.00 more altogether, in addition to the car. Colton eventually came home and once again could not believe I managed to get another car, as well as more money. We went up to Pine Ridge to pick up his stepfather, Philip. The three of us and the two full-grown Dobermans were headed back to Pennsylvania, in the very small car.

HERE I GO AGAIN

We were living in a motel at the entrance of Hickory Run State Park. I loved to go hiking while sometimes getting lost in the Pennsylvania forest. We had been at the motel for about a week when one day, out of the blue, there was a knock at the door. I was asked by the owner if I would consider managing the motel because the present manager had walked off the premises. As the new managers of the motel, we also received a free apartment. The owner was intrigued and in lust with Phillip. She called him over to her home nearly everyday for odd jobs. She was also the mayor of the small town.

During an argument, Colton kicked me in my tailbone so I was bedridden for a few days. I lost the job so we took Philip home and went to Pine Ridge. Colton took the car which was destroyed within a day. He cracked the block or something and we were without a car again. We were at his cousin Kent's house, when Colton pushed me down on a wheelchair ramp, grading a huge hunk of skin off of my knee and no one would medically help me. I needed stitches and the hospital turned me away because I was not a member of the tribe. Desperate, I went to the Catholic Church and spoke to the priest Robert, who helped me clean up my wound.

Robert had raised Colton's brother. As he was helping me, it was then that he told me Colton was too far gone in alcoholism to hope for repair.
I believed that love could conquer all. Colton and I decided to get married even though it was a small, informal ceremony by a judge at the Oglala Sioux Tribal courthouse. I will always remember the day, February 7th as being perfect, with blue skies filled with white puffy clouds. I was dressed in a long, black dress with lace sleeves and wore my witchy black cloak over it. Colton was wearing a black T-shirt and black jeans.

The day before, his aunt sold a very pretty watch to help us pay for the $20.00 marriage certificate. Colton's cousin Cody was his best man, while Cody's very drunk mother was our witness. She was so obnoxious that the judge had to keep telling her to keep quiet so we could get through the ceremony. I struggled hard to fit in on the Reservation. No matter how much I tried, the hard-core life on the Rez was too much for me. I thought my life had been hard to deal with thus far, but this experience proved me wrong. I made a friend who let me stay at his house when Colton would abuse me.

He was elderly and dying of cirrhosis of the liver. I pretty much became a live-in nurse for him. I didn't mind because I was friends with his niece across the street. So began my life alone on the Pine Ridge Reservation. I went and applied for a job at Yellow Birds convenience store. The woman who owned it was white and I think she hired me because she felt sorry for me. I felt that it was a miracle for me to be working at all. I was barely making minimum-wage, but I didn't mind. The hardest part about walking to work was being terrified of all the wild dogs.

I resumed communication with Dennis and found a small store over by the town of Kyle, where he could wire money to me through Western Union. It wasn't long before he agreed to buy me another car. If you don't have a car on the Rez, you end up having to hire someone with a car to take you wherever you need to go. I managed to hire a woman and her husband to give me a ride to Rapid City for $75.00. The couple and I went to a car lot where I found a Ford Tempo for $1400.00. I gave the salesman Dennis's phone number and he called him to attain his credit card number for the purchase.

With my new vehicle, I drove back down to Pine Ridge. I was very cautious while driving because the light was out on the license plate. I was going to pick up Colton and we were going to get off the Rez. Our plan was to go up to Keystone in the Black Hills, to work for the summer. I was upset that I could not return to work at the Red Garter Saloon until the owner came back from Mexico. Bewildered, I took a job at one of the two convenience stores in town as a clerk. I worked there for three weeks when I came up with the idea to take the day's earnings from the register. In the back of my mind, I wanted to go to jail; to be safe.

I think at this time in my life, I just wanted the roller coaster ride of abuse to end but I didn't know how to get off. I knew if the abuse continued, either he would end up killing me or worse, in defense I could end up killing him. Colton came from his job, to my work place around 11 pm. I told him that I would be closing the store shortly and to wait in the car. I also told him what I was planning to do.

It was raining hard and I remember looking out the window at him, sitting in the car with the dogs, waiting for me. I loved him but I couldn't take the mania of abuse in my life any longer. I think the way I felt could only be described as short-circuiting. I got several milk crates together and knew full well that I was on camera. I walked around the store and filled the crates with cartons of cigarettes, along with anything and everything we could possibly need in the near future.

I had three full crates by the time I was through. I even grabbed a few hundred lottery tickets. I then got all the money together and instead of dropping it into the safe, I put it into a deposit bag. I proceeded to set the alarm and had Colton help me carry out the crates, then turned around to lock the door behind me. I felt liberated. I told Colton to drive us to the spot where we always camped in the woods. I started going through the crates, showing him the loot I had gotten for us.

All of a sudden, like a lightning bolt, I realized I had forgotten the money bag. For a moment, Colton was trying to talk some sense into me, telling me to forget about it. I was determined to get the money so we could be well on our way, leaving the state of South Dakota once and for all. It was still pouring down rain by the time we pulled back into the parking lot in front of the store, around midnight. I told Colton to kill the lights and leave the engine running. I took a giant deep breath and put my key into the lock. I set off the very loud alarm, but I kept my cool. I walked around the counter, looked directly into the camera, grabbed the money bag and walked calmly out the door and re-locked it behind me.

Away we went, disappearing into the night. I knew it would take at least an hour before the sheriff would come and investigate from Rapid City. As Colton and I traveled through the night, I was scratching the lottery tickets. We cashed them in at different stores along the way. We ended up going back to South Dakota after a few months on the road. We found a mobile home for rent in Pine Ridge because the Rez is a great place to hide out if you are a fugitive. Serena had just given birth to another litter of puppies and Pagan was becoming even more aggressive because of the other dogs surrounding Serena outside of the house. Colton was always gone, drinking with his cousins. One night, I startled Pagan while he was sleeping and he viciously attacked me.

Before I knew what was happening, he had bitten large amounts of muscle and flesh from both of my calves, as well as from my left hip. I didn't know what to do because he nearly overpowered me. He could have ripped my throat out. All I could think of was how my own dog had turned against me with violence. He wasn't responding to my voice so I just said what was usually considered to be the magic phrase with both our dogs- Go for a ride in the car.

That seemed to snap him out of his attack mode. I hobbled to the door and let him jump in the car. He was acting happy, like nothing had happened. I didn't have a phone and I had no idea what to do, so I laid down for about an hour. This is when I started to realize with all the blood I lost, I was going into shock. I knew I had to do something fast. I went out to the car, allowing Pagan back into the house and I drove myself to the Indian Health Services Hospital.

I knew the white man's hospital and Gordon was too far away because the gas I had was not enough to get me that far. I wasn't even sure if I could make it without passing out. The priest that had helped me before was the one person who helped me to be seen. I was bleeding heavily from my wounds. The doctor stitching me up didn't really seem to know what he was doing. He was an older, white man. I feel sorry for the Lakota people, especially if all of their doctors were like this man.

159

The nurses were able to track Colton down for me and before long, he came and drove me home. I had crutches but I couldn't walk. Colton carried me around for a few weeks in the house.I returned to work, barely able to stand. I stole $400 from the register and went to where Colton was drinking with his cousins. I told him I was leaving because I desperately needed to get away from Pine Ridge. I asked him if he was going with me. Though he was drunk, he chose to be with his wife.

I loved the feeling of Colton and I being like Bonnie and Clyde, driving and being on the highway. Little did I know that the impending doom was just right around the corner although the temporary exhilaration seemed worth every bit of the adventure.

SIMPLE MAN

By the time we returned to Pennsylvania again, I knew something was not right with my sutures. I went to the hospital and was admitted because of a bad infection. Colton went to a friend's house that he had recently met to stay and visit. I was to be discharged and he was too intoxicated to come and pick me up. The situation was filled with unbelievable incompetence. I had sent my clothes with him when I was admitted so I had no clothing to wear whatsoever, even if I could find a ride.

Three, then four hours passed by. As a last resort I saw a preacher leaving the hospital and I ran out after him, wearing the hospital gown, along with a pair of scrub pants and those little booties. He gave me a ride to the campground where I used to camp. I was pissed about my situation with Colton. My friend gave me some clothes and we got high on a mixture of painkillers and weed, passing the night in a stupor.

The next day, I began to hunt my husband down as well as our car. When I found him I told him what an irresponsible imbecile he was but I still forgave him. Around September 11th, 2001 I was trying to mend my relationship with their father. He finally threw up the proverbial white flag and admitted he didn't want them anymore. Justin and Jeremy were now 11 and 12. I didn't waste time with excessive preparations. I jumped in my big, black, OJ Simpson looking Bronco and Colton and I were off.

After we arrived, we stayed in Tampa for a few days. The children had been living there for their entire lives and were never able to go to Busch gardens, so we went. I had a few thousand dollars, so we went to the local mall. Now, at 12 and 13 years old, they had never had a professional haircut and only raggedy-looking clothing- not the style of clothing and expensive sneakers that they desperately wanted. I wanted them to feel good about themselves so I bought them everything I could to make them feel like normal, happy, healthy children.

Once again, I explained to them that I still had to deal with Dennis a little bit more to get us into a house. I told Dennis we were going to live with him but a few days later I told him the children wanted it to just be me and them. He understood and gave me more money to find the suitable house. I was very choosy. I wanted to find a good school district in hopes that they could have a chance to get into a regular curriculum and not be considered for the need of special education.

I found an apartment in a good area but made the mistake of not choosing a home within town. The boys were already starving for interaction with other children when they came to me but didn't realize it until it was too late. In order to help them define their separate identities, I gave the only two bedrooms to each of them. Colton and I gave up privacy and allowed them to each have their own rooms.

I contacted the local middle school where the children would be attending. I began the process of trying to convince the administrators that my children deserved to have a chance to attend mainstream classes in their school. After a few interviews between me and the school board, along with reviewing the harmful environment the boys had come from as well as reading the reports from their previous schools in Florida, they were granted an admission interview. If it went well, they would be able to be placed into the regular curriculum.

Jeremy did great with his interview but Justin's interview did not go so well. He had a bad attitude that day and no matter how much I tried to coax him to at least fake being pleasant, it didn't work. He was therefore designated to attend a special needs school, which was for troubled kids and located nearly 40 miles away. It was an inconvenience but I was willing to go the extra distance for my son.

The afternoon after we filled out his entrance paperwork, I suppose it was just too much for him to deal with. When we got home, he punched out his bedroom window and was threatening to beat up Jeremy if he didn't quit making fun of him for not making it into his middle school. After I managed to get everything calmed down and cleaned up, I patched up the window the best I could from the inside and then had Colton climb on to the roof to not only to seal it from the outside but to decorate the windows with Christmas lights and to make the hole look like a big Christmas present to cover the missing glass.

I bought all of us nice and cozy warm Columbia coats and got the children geared up with gloves and hats, scarves and mittens. They were extra anxious for the snow to arrive. They had never seen it much less played in it. In the weeks ahead I continued to have meetings with the schools. The teachers could see all the damage that had been done by their father and they encouraged me to limit their contact with him. The children wanted to be free of their father but at the same time while struggling with their new life, it was hard to resist reverting back to their old, destructive patterns.

It was now my belief that if they were going to start the healing process and begin the path of a normal adolescence, I would have to deny the request for them to have contact with Stanley for a while. That would prove to cause everyone more harm than good.

Justin and Jeremy both began their school terms and at first were doing very well. I was so proud of them for their efforts. By the week of their Christmas vacation, I could feel that something bad was going to happen. So far in my life when I had a premonition like that, it usually fulfilled itself.

For Christmas, I didn't buy a lot more Christmas gifts for them because in the past few months I had already spent close to $20,000 tending to their needs and wants. They didn't care about all of that. The comment was even made that no matter what I do it will never be enough. Returning to school after their holiday vacation, I was informed that Jeremy really was not doing as good as I thought with adjusting to middle school. It was recommended that he attend Justin s school as a more suitable alternative. Jeremy didn't want to have to go there. He did not take it well. On the morning of the day I enrolled Jeremy into his new school, he began to display anger and an outburst emerged. The admissions counselor admonished him and told him that that type of behavior was unacceptable.

The entire ride home he was quiet. He went up to his room and slammed the door. Within minutes, he began screaming at me from the top of the stairs that he did not need a special school. He claimed that it was my fault he was placed into the special classes. Then came the destruction. He broke my cherished glass lamp, then proceeded to go throughout the house breaking window after window.

I tried and tried to restrain him. Colton was not there. At one point in the chaotic process, he broke my thumb as I had my arms wrapped around him from behind, trying to restrain him. When I let him go, he ran back upstairs, then climbed up onto the roof and was threatening to jump and kill himself.
I had an open warrant on me so I couldn't call the police I called Dennis. I didn't know what else to do. I walked Pagan and Serena down the road. I knew Dennis would be coming and thinking that if we were alone for a short time, he just might calm himself down a little.

I was quite frightened at this point. When I went back to the house, I did my best to comfort and hold Jeremy. Next, I told him that he was going to a special hospital for children to deal with the much needed help for dealing with mental health issues. I assured him that most likely there would be other kids there that were close to his age. Jeremy was admitted for a week. Before his release, the doctors wanted to prescribe Prozac for his moods to be stabilized. Regrettably, I refused the medication for him. The future may have turned out entirely different had I not made that decision.

After a long and drawn out, unproductive phone call with Rich, I asked him to relinquish sole custody of the children. At least grant me shared custody so I could get proper therapy or counseling for both of the children. He wouldn't budge.

BRIGHT LIGHTS

Colton left us a few days later to go back to South Dakota. He made sure to push me around and abuse me in front of the children, one last time, when yet again they chimed in with him, calling me derogatory names. I was emotionally drained. Jaxon decided he did not want to live with me anymore and wanted to go back to living with his dad. I called Rich and told him that Jeremy would be on a later flight back down to Tampa and to be at the airport when he arrived.

I just couldn't fight it all anymore. I was still battling depression and everything else that went with it. My heart was broken once again and I sobbed as I walked beside Jeremy through the entire length of the airport terminal. I knew I was not emotionally strong enough to heal my child. And his emotional baggage was too great for me to solve alone.

Almost a month had passed by when Justin and I packed up the house, rented a small U-Haul trailer and I withdrew him from school. Dennis loaned me his truck to tow it with. Justin had been talking to Colton and missed him terribly. So did I. We set out on the long, slow journey. I had to drive at 55 mph to keep the trailer from swaying.

As we made our way up through Nebraska, at last we came to the town of Rushville which is where I intended to find a place and get Justin enrolled in school. We checked into a motel that felt like it hadn't stepped out of the 1950's yet. After getting situated we were on our way, intent on going up to the Reservation to find Colton. As we drove intoWhite Clay, we found him- ten sheets to the wind. We had to plead with him to get into the truck. White Clay is a small town located right below the Reservation line that consists of buildings that sell at least 4 million cans of alcohol every year. It was a major contributor to the rampant alcoholism on the reservation

Millions of dollars of alcohol were sold to the natives because alcohol is illegal once you cross the state line. That comes out to around 4 million cans of beer and malt liquor. Nebraska cops would sit and wait for overly intoxicated drivers or whoever else that might have looked suspicious or easy to harass.Nebraska earned a sizable chunk of its revenue for the entire state on the short 20 mile stretch of two-lane highway between the reservation line and Rushville. If you wanted hard liquor, you had to go to Rushville.

As we went down the road to get back to Rushville, Colton began to act crazy and carried on about wanting to go back, so he jumped out and walked back to where he had been partying. Justin blamed me for Colton's refusal to come with us. He needed Colton, even though he was a major alcoholic. Upon returning to the motel, I stepped out for a moment, when Justin grabbed the keys, locked the doors and threatened to beat me down and take it. He was 13 at this time.

He was angry about everything but at the moment the biggest issue seemed to be that I needed to rest and couldn't take him out to the country roads so I could teach him how to drive. I had promised that we would do that. Justin then proceeded to call Rich and I had to defend my position as a mother once again as to why I thought moving out here would be beneficial for his education or rather what could be salvaged from it. Rich argued with me as usual. I told him I would call him back. I never did.

The following morning, I got up early and told Justin that I was going over to Chadron, Nebraska, located around 30 miles away. After that, I was going to take the back roads up to the Reservation to do laundry and see if I could find Colton. In truth, I needed a little time to myself to figure out what to do next. All seemed fine when I left. A little afternoon, as my laundry was finishing up. I called Rich and expected to be able to come up with some sort of resolution. Instead, I heard that the Nebraska sheriff's deputy and social services were at the motel room in Rushville. They also knew I had a warrant out for my arrest, and told me I needed to turn myself in.

My son had already been taken while all of my belongings and my beloved dogs remained in the room. I called the owner of the motel and played with her to be patient until Colton could come down and get the dogs in my possessions. She assured me that dogs were healthy and happy with an organization like the humane society and she would store my belongings. After finding Colton, I gave him a 50 dollar bill and told him to go down to Rushville to pick up the dogs. He got sidetracked of course, and had to buy booze and then he came back, he lied and said that he couldn't find the shelter where the dogs were located.

I was frantic about their whereabouts, in addition to everything else. A few more days had passed when somehow the dogs arrived in the front yard of where I was staying in Pine Ridge. I had no idea how anyone knew where I was located, much less where to bring the Doberman's. In the 2 weeks of my being separated from them, they had been tortured by being shot with a pellet gun, starved and left out in 0° weather. They were near death. They were indoor dogs.

It appeared that Pagan had been made to wear a muzzle the entire time. The saddest part was that Serena was pregnant and shot in her belly. How could people be so cruel? I really felt like I was approaching a serious nervous breakdown. I called Dennis and could not be comforted or consoled.

I borrowed antibiotics from everyone I knew and over the coming weeks, nursed my dogs back to health. In the meantime, Dennis came out and picked up his truck. Once again, I was alone again and had no car on the reservation. In the coming weeks, Colton and I went back to Pennsylvania. Dennis bought another car for me. Colton and I got a room in Hazleton.

Colton was obscenely drunk one night and even worse, smoking crack. He began knocking me around and because of the commotion, the motel owner called the police on us. Like the coward that he was, Colton ran out and into the woods. The cops ran the license plate on my car and then proceeded to arrest me. I was then extradited back to South Dakota by the Federal Marshals.

After arriving back in South Dakota, I was taken to the Pennington County Jail in Rapid City. Denys had eventually bailed me out and I took a bus back to him in Pennsylvania. He had my car and all of my belongings in his garage. He had been taking care of the dogs but they were now going to stay at his friend's house, until I arrived back because he had to leave for a short trip to visit his mother in Arizona.

It was pretty close to the dance season down in Daytona, so instead of waiting for Dennis to return from his trip, I left the same night I returned to head back down to Florida. I tried so hard to raise my spirits to be able to dance but just couldn't. I was devastated with sadness and sorrow. Here I was, trying to build up my self-esteem to perform and dance again but I was already defeated on the inside. I was truly losing my will to survive. I never did get to dance. It felt like I was at the lowest point of my life.

I was staying with an old Outlaw biker friend of mine who had a fenced yard, perfect for my dogs. I had to get Dennis to send me yet more money. By this time, the sum total of all the money he had given me was reaching near $100,000. After coming back from a shopping trip, Pagan and Serena were left alone in the car and Pagan won't let me in. He was acting vicious again and had, in his own dog's way, gone totally insane. He was having his own meltdown.

Animal control had to come to try to get him out. Instead they ended up shooting and killing him, as he lunged through the glass at them. I lost it and ran away. Serena was taken to a shelter. She was put down after a week of not being claimed by me. I passed a small storefront that was selling T-shirts. Within the hour, I was in the back room snorting huge lines of cocaine and posing nude for photographs. If you looked deep into my glassy eyes, you could have seen the pain which seeped from every pore in my body.

A day or two after, I was pulled over due to a busted out tail light, which in turn led to the warrant being discovered. Yes, the same warrant I had posted bail on had been issued because of my failure to appear at my court hearing in South Dakota for the convenience store robbery. Again, I was extradited by the U.S. Marshalls. I sat in the Pennington County jail for over 3 months waiting for my court hearing. Because it was considered my third theft felony, I was sentenced to a prison term of 3 years.

In South Dakota, the correctional system allows first-time offenders-prison inmates to only have to serve 25% of their time. I had already been granted credit for time served, so that only left around 9 months I would have to serve in prison before being granted parole. Not the worst, by far. After spending a few weeks in the fish tank, which refers to being locked in your room for 24 hours a day while they classify you, only going out for meals. I was soon classified into minimum status which allowed me to become a trustee.

Trustees lived in a separate building from the main prison and had much more freedom and benefits, including permission to work out in the community. I was excited to be moved out there for fresh air alone, after being in the fish tank for several weeks. I knew it would only be a matter of time before I would be working out in the real world. Exciting yes but it also scared me a little. I was still struggling with deep depression and I did not have a lot of confidence that I wouldn't run or something like that. It was an ominous and foreboding feeling.

Dennnis bought a television for me because it was considered to me to be an item of necessity because there were only two dumb radio stations in Pierre that didn't play up to date music. In the beginning of September, I was given an assignment to work for Game, Fish and Parks Service at Oahe Dam and Farm Island. I knew this would be the ultimate test. Would I pass? I knew myself and knew that the path I had been on did not consist predominantly of sensible choices.

Each and every morning before work, I would get up extra early and sit out front of the building on the bench while sipping on coffee and watching the South Dakota rise. The land surrounding the prison consisted of large and scenic rolling hills. It was beautiful if you pretended there wasn't a dump on the other side of those hills. Sometimes I would see horses or deer. One time I even saw a coyote which reminded me of days gone by when I still had my Pagan and Serena. I took the dogs to a regular spot to run off of a dirt road, located just outside of Rapid City. It was always a quick fix to allow them to get out and run and to be free for a while.

It was a very quiet evening and if I parked at the very top of one hill in particular, I could see cars coming from far in the distance so I knew I didn't have to worry about them. Pagan and Serena began running around and raising hell with the cows. It was funny because all of those cows headed up to where I was standing at the fence, more or less letting me know that Pagan was getting annoying.

Serena was off playing by herself. It was a gorgeous, full night and Pagan had disappeared for a while. Serena always stayed close to my side.
With the moon shining brightly down onto the rolling hills over the prairie, I could see a pack of coyotes in silhouette black forms. Low and behold, there was my Pagan, running right along with them. He was second to last; he must have demanded his way into the pack. My heart will never get over them being killed.

I felt at peace because I had been blessed to have Pagan and Serina come visit me in my dreams, running and playing just like that time, letting me know that they were okay and to ease my aching soul.
As I sat there contemplating my life, I prayed and pondered about my children too, sending them my love wherever they may be and hoping that they were doing good. I still couldn't help feeling dead inside even though it was my favorite season of the year.

When I first became a trustee and was waiting to be given an assignment, I was chosen to be on the Chainsaw Crew. If a disaster struck in the community, inmates from the men's prison and us women on the Crew would respond. We had to complete a chainsaw training program, where we learned how to dismantle the chainsaws and put them back together again. We also learned all of the important things that one needs to know on how to operate a chainsaw safely.

170

I was given the job of cutting a tree down while we were working at the dam. It felt so good to make a perfect wedge cut. Chopping cut wood for long periods of time is exhausting but I was the only one qualified for the job to operate the chainsaw. As the days began to pass, us workers began all working at the same work site instead of splitting up like usual.

We began to pick up cigarette butts and cigars. Occasionally, we got brave and went to the store which had an ashtray on the front porch. Technically, we were not supposed to go anywhere near the store.

Searching for butts like that felt humiliating. But alas! We are smoking and whether it was stale tobacco or not, it was good if we were to smoke again. Slightly humiliating though. One of the women had her friend drop off a few packs and we were in total bliss. A few weeks later she was to be released so I had Dennis send her some money through Western Union to buy a few cartons for me and to drop them off. I also needed other little luxuries that I had been deprived of for too long such as good hand lotion and lip gloss that tasted good instead of Carmex.

I also had to purchase Skoal and whatever else my coworkers wanted. I had to appease them for them to keep their traps shut. I didn't mind. I was simply thankful to not have to pick up butts off the ground anymore. Each day would bring some new adventure. The absolute grossest part of the job was the fish grinder. It was utterly disgusting. It was our responsibility to clean it and the surrounding areas.

Flies were always accumulating with maggots and that gave me the heebie-jeebies even more. The smell was gut-wrenching and horrible. I tried to reason with myself that all of the hard and nasty parts of the job balanced out with getting out every day into the fresh air and nature.

We would sometimes travel to maintain other parks in the area that weren't as occupied with residents and tourists. It was nice to see different scenery. At those Parks we mainly cleaned the restrooms and public areas. We would always find a way to sneak a cigarette, even if it was only worth a few drags. Our bosses knew what we were doing but they never said anything.

Dealing with life at the prison, I was starting to have a hard time at the end of each day while having to deal with everyday things that should not have bothered me as much as I allowed them to. I had a roommate who liked to sit bare ass naked on the only chair in the room when she got out of the shower. It was also very well known that she had a stinky athlete's foot. She always made a point to step on my bed in the middle bunk while going up to her bed on the top. Completely unnecessary.

In the Trustee building, there were very close living quarters. Throughout the entire prison was a one foot rule of separation throughout the area where you had to keep a distance of one foot between you and all other inmates. It was kind of a crazy rule considering that all three inmates in each room could not all be in there doing things at the same time, only sleep.

It was the end of September and I just can't seem to pull myself together and out of the slump I was in. Upon arriving at work one day, my friend Sophia and I requested a team up for jobs. We were told we were going to the archery range and would be working there all day. There were a lot of limbs and branches that had fallen from a recent storm. Each of us drove a variety of work-related vehicles at one time or another, depending on what job we were doing.

We mostly got around in the parks on a John Deere Gator. It was just the two of us that day along with the older boss whose name was Rodney. He was one of the three bosses and he was also a tenant of the park, designated as the host. Sophia and I got everything together and started out towards the archery range. The air was crisp and cool and we went off in opposite directions once we arrived. I was given a pole saw to start cutting the limbs. It is hard for a girl to hold and maneuver a saw like that above her head but I managed.

Before I really got engaged with work that morning, I sat down on the top of the hill on the mulch covered path while smoking a cigarette. I knew I was getting restless. I thought about asking the prison to pull me off of the job because I could feel some sort of temptation growing. That was just a dumb thought so I dismissed it quickly.

I was walking along the path, back to where I was to be cutting and came across wild plum bushes. They tasted divine. I grabbed a handful and sat back down cross-legged until I could not eat one more plum. Rodney had left us alone at the work site, which was kind of a No-No because we were to be supervised at all times by someone.

The gator was small enough that we could maneuver easily over the trails. I would cut away the excessive brush while she loaded it and then we tied it down with a chain. We then hauled it to a large truck in the parking lot to take it to the dump which was a great place to smoke. About mid-afternoon the Gator would not climb hills; actually it wasn't getting anywhere at all. We realized we had a flat tire. We took the truck back to the shop to try to find Rodney so we could tell him we needed to fix the tire but we couldn't find him.

We decided to go back to the work site to wait for him and continue on with our work, knowing that he would show up to check on us sooner or later. We all went back to the garage to search for another vehicle for us to complete our job for the day. After looking around for a few minutes at the four-wheeler possibilities, Rodney decided on one that had a flatbed for us. After removing a huge water tank off of the flatbed, Sophia and I began the trek back to the job site.

We had to go up and over a few hills but then we came to a huge hill that went straight down. Even though I shifted the gears properly, the brakes went out. We were careening fast, down the hill. Sophia had been riding on the flatbed and at about the halfway point down the hill, I shouted that we were going to need to jump. She protested for a second or two then I jumped. I landed hard on my left side then rolled a few times.

A few more seconds had passed before she finally jumped off, knocking her unconscious from her head hitting the ground so hard but then she quickly came to as I watched the vehicle, and disbelief to be down the hill. I thought for sure that when it hit the bottom of the ravine below it would cost an explosion but that did not happen thankfully. As we sat there trying to get ourselves calmed down, at first we were crying then the tears turned into laughter. When our legs were strong enough to walk again without shaking, we made our way to the top of the hill and started to call, "HELP!" for Rodney to hear, who was working close by.

The sheriff and ambulance were called to make a report and to seek medical attention for us. Right away, the medics put Sophia on a board with a stabilizing neck brace. Foolishly, I was afraid to admit I was hurt, so I told them that I was okay. I did not want to lose my job. I also refused to be taken to the hospital. I knew my spine was hurt and my hip was beginning to turn black from landing on it.

Sophia was taken to the hospital, while I took everyone to the scene of the accident to give a play-by-play description of how the event happened. It was a very bad decision to refuse medical attention. I could have and should have sued Game Fish and Parks for putting us on a faulty four-wheeler and jeopardizing our safety. We could have been killed.

When it was all over with and I was returned to the prison that evening, Sophia was still in the hospital. I was called to Health Services. The Major was waiting for me in the sitting area with papers to sign and for me to write out a statement about what happened. I was then told that I would have to remain on the prison grounds for 5 days of no work during the investigation.

My birthday came and went on the 9th of October which only seemed to add to my misery. The only consolation I had for myself was that I had not fulfilled my self-haunting prophecy of being dead by 33. I had been talking to Dennis nearly every day and he still continued to moan and whine about sex but now, he also talked about love and loving me and couldn't understand why I couldn't love him like he wanted and needed me to.

The day before I was to return to work, I received the findings of the accident report. It stated that I was at fault, which I am sure was to cover their asses, and ruled as a mere accident. I think every possible feeling at that moment was bubbling to the surface. I was about to overflow. I was put back on my job.

The only thing that made me feel better was knowing that Dennis was going to fly out to visit me so we could spend some time together while I was at work at the park. I would persuade him to buy me as many cartons of cigarettes as I wanted along with anything else I needed to get through the next few months. The weeks could not pass by quick enough. Dennis arrived on October 17th, which was a Friday, after flying into Minneapolis, Minnesota airport. He rented a car and drove the 8 hours it took to get to me in Pierre.

E Unit Trustee visits were from noon to 2 in the afternoon. I didn't know I could have requested a Special Visit which would have lasted for 4 hours but he didn't care as long as he could touch me and tell me how much he wanted to have sex with me. All I cared about was for him to get straight to the list of things I wanted. Just to pacify him a bit, I told him to go and buy a sexy outfit for me to slip into. I went on to tell him that it would give us a better chance to cruise around the park without drawing too much attention to my bright orange T-shirt which had inmate printed on the back of it.

I then also made him a feeble promise that we would at least have a quickie-only after he gave me the bag of stuff I requested and only after he drove me to the area where I needed to go in the park in order to conceal it. I knew what time we arrived at the shop each morning and told Denniss where to park the car so that I could easily meet him on Monday morning. He was ecstatic! At the end of our visit, he hugged me and whispered in my ear, " I can't wait." It made my stomach lurch and turn a little sickly.

On Monday morning, October 20th, at 8:20 am, I got out of the work van and walked into the shop as always and went directly to my locker to get my cigarettes. I then walked straight out of the building- I'm sure my coworkers thought I was simply going for an early smoke even though we usually waited until we were at our designated job sites. I didn't really care what they thought. I knew in a few hours they would all be kissing up to me, knowing I had all the loot and goods that we could possibly want.

As I walked around the building, my heart began to race so I lit a cigarette. With hurried steps, I made my way through the small patch of woods. It was gray and damp and cold but I felt at peace. As I emerged from the trees- there was Dennis, parked right where I told him to park.

I ran up to the car and jumped in and gave him a quick kiss before crouching down. As he was driving around the park, I stripped naked and put on the outfit that he had bought for me. We took the bags of stuff to the edge of the park. The park was mostly uninhabited because of the time of year. I was still very paranoid that I had taken too much time to " smoke, "though in reality, it couldn't have been more than 10 minutes since I had disappeared.

I really wanted to get back to the shop. I told Dennis that he would have to wait until I was released before we could have the sex he so desperately wanted. He was very upset that he had come so far and was leaving with nothing but kisses. I tried to reason with him but the effort was futile. After a few minutes, I began to panic. I knew if I was caught in the car I would be going straight to the hole upon return at the prison. I would lose everything and some of the freedom that I had so far.

I finally felt like I was getting my head a little above the water and wanted to continue to get healthy and my mind, body and spirit. When I was released, I could easily support myself and thrive, not just survive anymore. Dennis did not care about that. The only thing he cared about was getting his dick wet. At that moment, I hated him so much.

Worse yet, I hated myself more. Internally, something shattered. Still feeling like I was standing on the edge of that cliff, the proverbial thread I was hanging onto broke. Or maybe I just let go. How could I let this man make me feel cheap and like a whore?

I climbed into the backseat, laid down flat then lit a cigarette and told him to fucking drive and to keep driving out of the park! Then I instructed him to follow my directions to get to the back way to the Interstate. He was not to stop until I was far away from South Dakota. If I had a gun, it would have been held to his head. It felt like there was no turning back, whether I wanted to or not.

Peace and Love,

Selira

SOMETIMES IT'S A BITCH

Well I've run through rainbows
and castles of candy
I've cried a river of tears from the pain
I've tried to dance with what life had to hand me
My partner's been pleasure
My partner's been pain…

Sometimes It's a Bitch
Sometimes It's a Breeze
Sometimes It's Roses
Sometimes It's Weeds
Sometimes It's A Bitch
Sometimes It's A Breeze…

AUTHOR BIO

Selira V. Samanne lives just outside the beautiful mountain town of Nederland Colorado, elevation 8,245 ft nestled just above Boulder. She has lived in Boulder County since 2016 and has truly found the place she has always been searching for: to have a place to call home, a place to be and a sense of belonging and community. She lives with her two Black Lab canine companions, Pagan and Tarot. She loves spending time deep in the wilderness while taking in the sights of wildlife like moose, bear, elk and mountain lions while being at peace in the serenity of the forest.

CHAPTER SONG TITLES	HAIR-BAN NAMES

HELL IS FOR CHILDREN
PAT BENATAR

RAINBOW IN THE DARK
DIO

BIG BALLS
AC/DC

METAL HEALTH
QUIET RIOT

WE'RE NOT GOING TO TAKE IT
TWISTED SISTER

ROUND AND ROUND
RAT

GYPSY ROAD
CINDERELLA

HEAVEN'S ON FIRE
KISS

CRY TOUGH
POISON

YOUTH GONE WILD
SKID ROW

COMING OF AGE
DAMN YANKEES

NO ONE LIKE YOU
SCORPIONS

WILD SIDE
MOTLEY CRUE

FALLEN ANGEL
POISON

WHEREVER I MAY ROAM
METALLICA

ONCE BITTEN TWICE SHY
GREAT WHITE

BRINGING ON THE HEARTBREAK
(Version 1)
DEF LEPPARD

ESTRANGED
GUNS AND ROSES

GIRLS GIRLS GIRLS
MOTLEY CRUE

NO MORE TEARS
OZZY OSBOURNE

KICKSTART MY HEART
MOTLEY CRUE

ROAD TO NOWHERE
OZZY OSBOURNE

FAR BEHIND
CANDLEBOX

HELLRAISER
OZZY OSBOURNE

GONE AWAY
THE OFFSPRING

WHAT YOU GIVE
TESLA

ROCKSTAR
NICKELBACK

WONDERFUL
EVERCLEAR

HERE I GO AGAIN
WHITESNAKE

SIMPLE MAN
SHINEDOWN

BRIGHT LIGHTS
MATCHBOX 20

SOMETIMES IT'S A BITCH
STEVIE NICKS

REVIEW

Selira V. Samanne's tumultuous life experience is vividly and authentically depicted in Experience From Midnight. This gripping story provides an honest and unvarnished look at the difficulties faced by a young girl who had to navigate the harsh reality of the streets to flee abuse. Selira's unwavering spirit is evident on every page, navigating both the trials of youth and the perils of adulthood.

A must read for anybody looking for motivation and insight into the resilience of the human spirit is Journey from Midnight.

Haleemah Begum

Reviewed in the United Kingdom